Greenhave

20.9

P.O. 67128

DISCARDED

Legalized Gambling

OTHER BOOKS OF RELATED INTEREST

OPPOSING VIEWPOINTS SERIES
Alcohol
American Values
America's Prisons
Chemical Dependency
Crime and Criminals
Criminal Justice
The Legal System
The War on Drugs

CURRENT CONTROVERSIES SERIES
Alcoholism
Crime
Gambling
Native American Rights

Legalized
Gambling

David L. Bender, *Publisher*
Bruno Leone, *Executive Editor*
Bonnie Szumski, *Editorial Director*
Brenda Stalcup, *Managing Editor*
Scott Barbour, *Senior Editor*
Mary E. Williams, *Book Editor*

Contemporary Issues
Companion

Greenhaven Press, Inc., San Diego, CA

Every effort has been made to trace the owners of copyrighted material. The articles in this volume may have been edited for content, length, and/or reading level. The titles have been changed to enhance the editorial purpose. Those interested in locating the original source will find the complete citation on the first page of each article.

Library of Congress Cataloging-in-Publication Data

Legalized gambling / Mary E. Williams, book editor.
    p.   cm. — (Contemporary issues companion)
    Includes bibliographical references and index.
    ISBN 1-56510-898-1 (pbk : alk. paper). — ISBN 1-56510-899-X
(lib. : alk. paper)
    1. Gambling—United States. 2. Gambling—Law and legislation—United States. 3. Compulsive gambling—United States. 4. Gambling on Indian reservations—United States. I. Williams, Mary E.,
1960–   . II. Series
HV6715.L43 1999
363.4'2'0973—dc21   98-11807
                                                                    CIP

©1999 by Greenhaven Press, Inc.
P.O. Box 289009, San Diego, CA 92198-9009

Printed in the U.S.A.

CONTENTS

FOREWORD

In the news, on the streets, and in neighborhoods, individuals are confronted with a variety of social problems. Such problems may affect people directly: A young woman may struggle with depression, suspect a friend of having bulimia, or watch a loved one battle cancer. And even the issues that do not directly affect her private life—such as religious cults, domestic violence, or legalized gambling—still impact the larger society in which she lives. Discovering and analyzing the complexities of issues that encompass communal and societal realms as well as the world of personal experience is a valuable educational goal in the modern world.

Effectively addressing social problems requires familiarity with a constantly changing stream of data. Becoming well informed about today's controversies is an intricate process that often involves reading myriad primary and secondary sources, analyzing political debates, weighing various experts' opinions—even listening to firsthand accounts of those directly affected by the issue. For students and general observers, this can be a daunting task because of the sheer volume of information available in books, periodicals, on the evening news, and on the Internet. Researching the consequences of legalized gambling, for example, might entail sifting through congressional testimony on gambling's societal effects, examining private studies on Indian gaming, perusing numerous websites devoted to Internet betting, and reading essays written by lottery winners as well as interviews with recovering compulsive gamblers. Obtaining valuable information can be time-consuming—since it often requires researchers to pore over numerous documents and commentaries before discovering a source relevant to their particular investigation.

Greenhaven's Contemporary Issues Companion series seeks to assist this process of research by providing readers with useful and pertinent information about today's complex issues. Each volume in this anthology series focuses on a topic of current interest, presenting informative and thought-provoking selections written from a wide variety of viewpoints. The readings selected by the editors include such diverse sources as personal accounts and case studies, pertinent factual and statistical articles, and relevant commentaries and overviews. This diversity of sources and views, found in every Contemporary Issues Companion, offers readers a broad perspective in one convenient volume.

In addition, each title in the Contemporary Issues Companion series is designed especially for young adults. The selections included in every volume are chosen for their accessibility and are expertly edited in consideration of both the reading and comprehension levels of the audience. The structure of the anthologies also enhances accessibility. An introductory essay places each issue in context and provides helpful facts such as historical background or current statistics and legislation that pertain to the topic. The chapters that follow organize the material and focus on specific aspects of the book's topic. Every essay is introduced by a brief summary of its main points and biographical information about the author. These summaries aid in comprehension and can also serve to direct readers to material of immediate interest and need. Finally, a comprehensive index allows readers to efficiently scan and locate content.

The Contemporary Issues Companion series is an ideal launching point for research on a particular topic. Each anthology in the series is composed of readings taken from an extensive gamut of resources, including periodicals, newspapers, books, government documents, the publications of private and public organizations, and Internet websites. In these volumes, readers will find factual support suitable for use in reports, debates, speeches, and research papers. The anthologies also facilitate further research, featuring a book and periodical bibliography and a list of organizations to contact for additional information.

A perfect resource for both students and the general reader, Greenhaven's Contemporary Issues Companion series is sure to be a valued source of current, readable information on social problems that interest young adults. It is the editors' hope that readers will find the Contemporary Issues Companion series useful as a starting point to formulate their own opinions about and answers to the complex issues of the present day.

INTRODUCTION

The Rescue Mission in Atlantic City, New Jersey, provides food, clothing, and shelter for more than three thousand indigent people each year. Because it receives more than one million dollars in donations annually from the city's casinos, the mission faces no difficulties accommodating the needs of all who ask for help. Many of these needy, however, are problem or compulsive gamblers who have lost all of their money at the casinos—and therein lies what several commentators see as the central irony of the mission. "If the casinos weren't here, you wouldn't need a mission this size," states Barry K. Durman, the mission's chief executive, in a 1998 *New York Times* article by Brett Pulley. "And if the casinos weren't supporting us," Durman continues, "we wouldn't be able to serve the number of people we serve."

For many observers, the Atlantic City Rescue Mission illustrates the best as well as the worst aspects of America's latter twentieth-century gambling boom. Supporters of legalized betting contend that the growth of gambling venues has resulted in enhanced tourism, job opportunities, and financial profits that have provided much-needed revenue for many communities. Others maintain, however, that the spread of gambling has led to an increase in compulsive behavior as well as higher rates of bankruptcy, crime, violence, and family deterioration.

Americans have had mixed feelings about betting since colonial times. Gambling proved hard to curb in spite of a 1630 law that criminalized games of chance. The original thirteen colonies, in fact, eventually instituted lotteries to raise finances, some of which helped to fund some of the nation's private colleges, including Harvard, Princeton, and Yale. Legal and illegal lotteries flourished early in the nineteenth century, and by 1830, lotteries were making an estimated sixty million dollars annually. In the 1890s, however, public outcry about corruption in the Louisiana state lottery spurred Congress to pass the Federal Lottery Act, which limited interstate mailing of printed lottery materials.

Casino gambling, also popular in the nineteenth century, prospered along the Atlantic coastline and on the Mississippi and Ohio Rivers, moving westward as new territories opened up. Sentiment against betting was strong, too, and many gambling enthusiasts were frightened away from southern river towns after the 1835 lynching of five gamblers in Natchez, Mississippi. Despite this antigambling fervor, riverboat gaming bounced back in the 1840s, with nearly two thousand professional gamblers plying their skills along the Mississippi River. Casinos thrived in the western states also, particularly in Nevada. Although prohibitionists outlawed gambling in Nevada early in the twentieth century, antigaming laws were rarely enforced, and in 1931—prompted by a need to stimulate the state's economy during the depression—Nevada passed laws allowing most forms of gambling. During that same year, Massachusetts legalized bingo, and in 1933, New Hampshire, Michigan, and Ohio decriminalized betting pools for horse races and dog races.

A series of events set the stage for the modern gambling era. In 1964, New Hampshire voters approved a state-sponsored lottery. In 1976, New Jersey legalized gambling in Atlantic City. Between 1980 and 1990, twenty-five states ratified lotteries as well as off-track betting, video poker, and keno. A Supreme Court decision in 1987 enabled American Indian tribes to open gaming establishments in states that allowed gambling. By 1998, Utah and Hawaii were the only two states that had not legalized some form of gambling.

Despite this dramatic expansion of legal gambling, Americans remain ambivalent about casinos and lotteries.

Gambling's supporters contend that legalized gambling has provided economic boosts for many communities through increased tourism, jobs, and casino and lottery revenues. Tunica County, Mississippi, is often cited as an example of the beneficial effects of gambling. In 1982, the U.S. Department of Commerce declared Tunica County the poorest in the nation, with a per capita income of less than six thousand dollars. By 1994—two years after the first of Tunica's riverboat casinos opened—the per capita income had increased to nearly eleven thousand dollars. That year, the jobless rate dropped to an all-time low of 4.9 percent, according to Alan Salomon, a reporter for *Advertising Age*. In 1993, Tunica County's casinos employed ten thousand workers; by 1994, twenty-eight thousand people worked in the casinos. The Mississippi state government received a budgetary surplus in excess of three hundred million dollars in 1993, 35 percent of it attributable to gaming, claims Denton Gibbs, a state public relations director. Because of this budgetary windfall, Gibbs contends, Mississippi now has enough money to repair bridges, improve roads, and enlarge highways. Furthermore, state officials maintain, the presence of the casinos has stimulated growth in the local hotel, advertising, and retail businesses.

Beyond gambling's economic incentives, many commentators argue that the spread of gambling has given more consumers needed access to a form of recreation that contrasts sharply with the increasingly alienating world of work and entertainment. Gerri Hirshey, contributing writer to the *New York Times Magazine*, states that "as workplaces become more isolationist—setting us in computer stations, telemarketing carrels, home offices—entertainment itself has become less communal, more remote." For example, she claims, "in 1993, for the first time, the solitary pursuits of video games outsold movie admissions. . . . Nineteen ninety-four's Woodstock II concert [generated] $20 million in pay-per-view revenues from couch potato communards. How, then, can anyone profess surprise at the casinos' staggering numbers? They're one of the few ways left to experience Saturday night *live*, to get out amid squealing, yee-hawing humans determined to raise a wee tad o' heck."

Those who remain concerned about the spread of gambling, however, do not agree that these economic and social incentives outweigh gambling's potential harms. Several commentators argue, for example, that Tunica County's prospects are not as rosy as state officials have claimed. "The casinos have not rescued Tunica's poor," authors Benjamin and Christina Schwarz maintain. "Although [the county] now has more jobs than residents, most of those jobs, particularly the better-paying ones, have gone to people from outside the county." Moreover, the Schwarzes point out, the September 1995 unemployment rate in Tunica County was 13.6 percent—nearly twice the average for the state of Mississippi—so that the county continues to have one of the highest unemployment rates in the nation. Other critics argue that an influx of casinos into a locality often harms already-existing restaurants and shops by steering consumers' money away from non-gaming businesses.

The primary argument against gambling is that casino proliferation has led to an increase in compulsive gambling, a disease similar to alcoholism and drug addiction. This increase in compulsive gambling, in turn, has resulted in higher rates of bankruptcy, theft, and embezzlement in and around gambling locales, many commentators argue. Jeffrey L. Bloomberg, state attorney for Lawrence County, South Dakota, attributes growing crime rates in his county to casino proliferation in the area: "We have seen individuals who, prior to their exposure to gambling, had no criminal history. They were not junkies or alcoholics; many of them had good jobs; they became hooked on slot machines, and after losing all their assets, . . . began committing some type of crime to support their addiction." Most disturbing, perhaps, is a University of California study that found that suicide rates in Atlantic City, Las Vegas, and Reno are nearly four times higher than in comparably sized non-gambling cities. Other studies have associated higher rates of white-collar crime, child abuse, and substance abuse with gambling, claims sociologist David Phillips, conductor of the UC study.

Gambling is now one of the most popular forms of recreation in America; at the same time, opposition to gambling appears to be gaining strength, as evidenced by the numerous failed post-1994 proposals to legalize gaming at the state level. *Legalized Gambling: Contemporary Issues Companion* illuminates this national ambivalence as it investigates the world of wagering, provides several individual perspectives on gambling, examines the controversies surrounding gambling's societal effects, and explores the issue of Indian gaming.

CHAPTER 1

THE WORLD OF GAMBLING

LEGALIZED GAMBLING: A HISTORY

Richard McGowan

Richard McGowan traces the history of U.S. gambling from the state-sanctioned lotteries of the seventeenth century to the dramatic rise of casinos in the late twentieth century. While legalized gambling has often served as a lucrative source of income for states, private parties, and nonprofit institutions, its popularity has stirred controversy, McGowan points out. He describes, for example, how scandals involving dishonest operators and rigged games occasionally prompt the banning of some forms of betting. Moreover, the author notes, critics argue that gaming should be curbed because it preys on compulsive gamblers and the poor, while supporters contend that an individual's right to gamble should be protected. McGowan, the author of *State Lotteries and Legalized Gambling: Painless Revenue or Painful Mirage*, teaches economics at Boston College in Chestnut Hill, Massachusetts.

In 1984, all forms of gambling (lotteries, race tracks, casinos, and other forms of legalized betting) accounted for less than $15 billion in revenues. In 1995, these gaming activities generated $55.3 billion in revenues, nearly a 400 percent increase in eleven years. The surge in gaming activity in the United States has many social observers searching for reasons why gambling has become so socially acceptable. Gambling, particularly casino gambling, has become a means of salvation in terms of economic development for troubled urban areas ranging from Chicago to New Bedford, Massachusetts. But this interest in gambling as a method of raising revenue for states and providing economic relief for depressed areas is hardly unique in American history.

Four "waves" of state-sponsored gambling activity have occurred in U.S. history.

The First Wave: State-Sanctioned Lotteries

The first wave of gaming activity (1607–1840s) in the United States began with the landing of the first settlers but became much more widespread with the outbreak of the Revolutionary War. During this time, lotteries were the approved form of gaming. A few were spon-

From Richard McGowan, "The Rise of Casino Gambling." This article appeared in the March 1997 issue and is reprinted with permission from *The World & I*, a publication of The Washington Times Corporation, copyright ©1997.

sored by states to help finance their armies, but most were operated by
nonprofit institutions such as colleges, local school systems, and hospitals to finance building projects or needed capital improvements.

For example, both Yale and Harvard (this rivalry started much earlier than football!) used lotteries to build dormitories. In 1747, the
Connecticut legislature gave Yale a license to raise 7,500 pounds,
while Harvard had to wait until 1765 to win approval from the Massachusetts legislature to conduct a lottery worth 3,200 pounds. Harvard's was much less successful than Yale's, primarily because it had to
compete with lotteries supporting troops fighting the French and
Indian War.

During this wave of lottery activity, no state ever operated its own
lottery. They were conducted by private operators after an organization or a worthy project such as the Erie Canal had received permission from state legislatures to do so.

These private operators of lotteries often proved less than honest,
however. One famous scandal occurred in Washington, D.C., in 1823.
Congress authorized a Grand National Lottery to pay for improvements to the city. Tickets were sold and the drawing took place, but
before the winners could collect, the private agent who organized the
lottery fled town with the money. While the majority of winners
accepted their fate with resignation, the winner of the $100,000
grand prize sued the D.C. government, and the Supreme Court ruled
that the city had to pay.

It was a sober reminder to local officials that authorizing lotteries
could be dangerous, and the movement to ban lotteries began. From
1840 to 1860, all but two states prohibited lottery activity due to various scandals that occurred in the 1820s and '30s. However, it would
take less than forty years for lotteries to once again explode on the
national scene.

The Second Wave: National Lotteries

With the conclusion of the Civil War in 1865, the South had to find
some method to finance the reconstruction of roads, bridges, school
buildings, and various other social capital projects damaged in the
war. The victorious North was in no mood to provide for its defeated
cousins. Hence, southern legislatures allowed private operators to
conduct lotteries to raise these sorely needed funds.

The primary difference between this period of lottery activity and
the previous one is the scale of ticket sales. Whereas before sales were
confined to local regions, these southern lotteries took on a national
scope and ironically were particularly popular in the North. The most
famous of these, conducted in Louisiana, was known as the Serpent.
At the height of this lottery in the late 1880s, almost 50 percent of all
mail coming into New Orleans was connected with it.

As happened with lotteries in the previous period, controversy eventually led the federal government to ban the Serpent. In 1890, the charter authorizing the lottery in Louisiana was about to expire. Lottery operators bribed various state officials with offers of up to $100,000 to reinstate it. The rather flagrant method they used to ensure that the Serpent's charter would be reinstated was reported throughout the country. This led various state legislatures to pass resolutions calling on Congress and President Benjamin Harrison to stop the Serpent. There can be little doubt that these legislatures were most upset because out-of-state sales of Louisiana lottery tickets amounted to over $5 million per year. Harrison urged Congress to pass legislation to curb all lottery activity.

The primary way to cripple the Louisiana lottery was to deny it the use of the federal mail system. If customers could no longer mail in their requests for tickets, then the lottery would be short-lived. In late 1890, Congress banned the use of federal mails for lottery sales. By 1895, the Serpent had vanished, and, as the new century dawned, gaming activity in the United States had ceased to exist. But like a phoenix, lotteries as well as other forms of gaming would again be resurrected as government searched for additional sources of revenue in the late twentieth century.

The Third Wave: State-Operated Lotteries

While many states started to permit pari-mutuel betting on horse races, dog races, or jai-alai in the 1920s and Nevada legalized casino gambling in the 1930s, gambling generally remained a socially unacceptable activity from 1900 to the mid-1960s. However, in 1964, New Hampshire voters approved a lottery, the form of gaming that had been adopted by the previous waves of gaming. The rationale used to justify its legalization was strictly economic. Proceeds from the lottery were to fund education, thereby averting the enactment of either a sales or income tax for New Hampshire. The lottery was an instant success, with 90 percent of the lottery tickets being bought by out-of-state residents.

This lesson was not lost on neighboring states. In the next ten years, every northeastern state approved a lottery. Two rationales were used to justify lottery activity in all these states: (1) People are going to gamble, so why shouldn't the state profit from this activity? (2) The neighboring state is reaping benefits from our constituents, so we need to institute a lottery to keep the money "home." This time the lotteries were operated by state agencies. They were not only state-sanctioned but owned and operated by state governments.

The greatest growth of state lotteries occurred between 1980 and 1990. During this time, twenty-five states approved not only lotteries but other forms of gambling, such as off-track betting (OTB), keno (a type of high-stakes bingo that is played every five minutes), and video poker machines (usually found in bars and restaurants). All these new forms were meant to supplement the revenue capabilities of lotteries. By 1993, only two states (Utah and Hawaii) did not have some form of legalized gaming. Lotteries and associated forms of gaming had gained a social acceptance that had not occurred in previous waves.

Gambling as a Source of Revenue

Four quite pronounced differences distinguish this third wave of gambling from the previous two. First is the widespread use of gambling as a source of revenue for state governments. Thirty-eight states plus the District of Columbia sponsor a lottery. Ironically, the South is the only section of the country that has so far withstood the lottery craze, but it also spends the least amount of tax dollars on social and welfare projects.

Second, the depth of gambling taking place is unprecedented. No longer is the lottery being confined to a monthly or even weekly drawing. Most states offer three types of games. A daily number game involves selecting a three- or four-digit number for a fixed-amount prize. The "lotto," in which 6 numbers of a possible 40 or 48 are picked, is usually played twice a week, and jackpots can build up to sums as high as $90 million. The final innovation was the "instant" or scratch tickets. In all these games, the players know immediately if they have won. Also, the odds and the size of the prize for these games can vary greatly. The other striking feature of this third wave is states' willingness to engage in several types of gambling activities, such as keno, video poker, and off-track betting.

The third difference between the current wave and previous waves is not only state sponsorship but state ownership of lottery operations. Whereas before, the actual operation of the lottery was given to private brokers, now the state itself is the operator and sole beneficiary. True, some states—Georgia, Nebraska, West Virginia, and Maine, for example—have permitted private concerns such as Scientific Games and G-Tech to operate the instant game portion of their lotteries, but the vast majority of lottery operations are conducted by the states themselves.

There can be little doubt that the downfall of many previous lotteries was due in great measure to the scandal-ridden operations of the private brokers commissioned by the state. However, even state-operated lotteries are not immune to scandals. In the early 1980s, Pennsylvania's daily number drawing was exposed as being rigged—certain balls were heavier than others, accounting for the famous winning number 666.

The final difference concerning this third wave of lottery activity relates to the supposedly "good" causes that the proceeds are used to support. In the previous waves, profits supported were one-time events such as the building of canals, bridges, and highways. Once the cause was completed, then the lottery ceased. The state did not depend on lottery proceeds to fund ongoing services that constituents expected the state to provide.

In the third wave, state lottery proceeds support activities that the public has traditionally expected the state to fund continuously. Many states—such as California, Illinois, Florida, and New Jersey— also use lottery proceeds to fund education (note that these funds are not "supplements" to build new schools, and so forth, but are regular support for the day-to-day operations of the schools). In other states, lottery proceeds fund Medicare (Pennsylvania) and support police and fire departments in local communities (Massachusetts) as well as a host of daily government operations.

In other words, state lotteries are no longer a "one shot" affair. They must be able to provide the state with a consistent source of revenue to fund the various "good" causes that their supporters insist that they can.

However, the vast majority of state lotteries have not been able to provide this consistent source of revenue. Lottery games were subject to what is known as the product life cycle, that is, sales increase at first but later the demand for lottery tickets gradually decreases. Sales of daily number tickets have been declining in almost every state that operates a lottery. This is true even in Massachusetts, which operates the most successful lottery in the nation.

Meanwhile, lotto sales have been subject to "jackpot fatigue," such that interest can be generated only when jackpots exceed $15 million. To overcome this phenomenon, states have joined together to build jackpots more quickly. But clearly lotto games are not a consistent source of income for revenue-hungry states. The one lottery game that seems to be able to achieve a slow increase in sales is the instant game segment, but this is of little consolation to legislators who need to find a source of revenue that can finance needed social services. It is precisely because lotteries have been unable to provide more revenue that states are turning to another form of gaming, whose potential seems to be much more elastic, namely casino gambling.

The Fourth Wave: The Triumph of Casino Gaming

In 1993, for the first time in U.S. gaming history, revenues from casino gaming were greater than those from lotteries. This marked a turning point: Casino gambling became the preferred form of gaming in the United States. It also marked a turning point in our acceptance of gambling as a legal source of entertainment. Finally, this development returns the control of gaming operations to private concerns, since casinos are owned and operated by private corporations (although they are certainly heavily regulated by the states).

By 1995, casino gambling had completely surpassed lotteries as the preferred form of gaming. That year, total gaming revenues in the United States were $55.3 billion—with nearly 60 percent going to casino operators, while state lotteries took in 28 percent and the rest went to pari-mutuel betting and charitable gaming.

How did this expansion of casino gaming take place? There is a three-part explanation. First, during the late 1980s the two "traditional" markets for casino gambling, Las Vegas and Atlantic City, transformed themselves from strictly casino operations to "family-oriented" vacation centers. For example, MGM's Las Vegas operations were renewed by building a theme park beside a newly renovated casino operation. In Atlantic City, casino operators were able to add hotel rooms as well as receive relief from various regulations concerning their operations. The threat that Pennsylvania might permit riverboat gaming persuaded New Jersey legislators to protect their casino industry. Overall, these two locations experienced a 22 percent increase in gaming revenues and a 24 percent increase in visitors during the early 1990s.

Second, a new form of casino gambling, riverboat gambling, became popular in the 1990s. In 1989, Iowa became the first state to permit it, soon to be followed by Louisiana, Illinois, Indiana, Mississippi, and Missouri. It is interesting to note that all these states had lotteries except for Mississippi. Why this turn to riverboat gambling? Because these states had experienced a decrease in lottery sales, and riverboat gambling seemed like a good source of revenue that had not been tapped and could replace the revenue that their lotteries were now losing.

Third are the Indian casino gaming operations. In 1988, Congress passed the Indian Gaming Regulatory Act (IGRA), which permitted Indian tribes to develop casinos and bingo parlors into major economic centers. By far, the most successful Indian casino has been Foxwoods in Connecticut, which is the world's largest casino, generating nearly $800 million in 1995. Its revenues exceeded the state's lottery revenues that year. This fact has not been lost on state legislators. Massachusetts, whose lottery contributes nearly $800 million to state coffers, has invited one of its Indian tribes to set up a casino in New Bedford, an economically depressed area in southeastern Massachusetts, to compete with the Foxwoods casino in Connecticut. Since 1988, some 124 Indian casino facilities, ranging from bingo halls to full-fledged casinos such as Foxwoods, have sprouted in twenty-four states. Revenues from Indian casinos now exceed those from state lotteries.

Casino gambling has clearly become the dominant force behind a virtual explosion of gaming activity in the United States. While casino gaming will continue to spread into new jurisdictions, the rate at which additional states authorize casino gaming will certainly slow but will continue for three reasons, which parallel the rationale for the growth in lotteries. First, taxes and economic activity generated by casino gaming will be appreciated as the states are saddled with the cost of various programs previously funded by the federal government. Second, a state that does not have casino gaming risks losing a lot of potential tourist and tax revenue to a neighboring state that does. Third, while recent elections have shown that voters often view casino gaming as a NIMBY (Not In My Backyard), it is ironic that the vast majority of Americans want the "right" to gamble and view gambling as another form of entertainment that should be available to anyone who wishes to engage in it.

Obviously, this broad acceptance of gambling (particularly casino gaming) is a new development in America. Both of the first two waves of gambling activity ended because the public would no longer condone the social costs associated with even lottery operations. Meanwhile, since 1964 not only has the public tolerated greatly increased lottery activity but it now seems to be demanding the right to participate much more extensively.

Societal Good Versus Individual Rights

Even with the widespread acceptance of gambling, the start of casino gambling has been surrounded by controversy. Invariably, the controversy involves a conflict between those who insist that the goal of public policy should be to maintain the "societal good" and those who advocate the supremacy of the "rights of the individual."

Those who advocate the institution of casino gambling appeal to a very different ethical argument. They contend that people are natural gamblers and will do so whether or not the government allows it. Therefore, since people are going to gamble anyway, shouldn't government legalize it as long as the proceeds are used for a "good" purpose? After all, government cannot legislate morality.

Meanwhile, those who oppose the adoption of casino gambling usually invoke the argument that it preys on the poor or those who become addicted to gambling. Therefore, it is in the best interest of "society" that lotteries and gambling be outlawed. They maintain that society cannot permit any activity that feeds the addiction of some segment even if the rest of society might derive benefit.

Historically, numerous public-policy debates in the United States—such as slavery, taxation, and states' rights—have focused on this conflict between "the societal good" and "the rights of the individual." Even today this conflict governs the debate on issues ranging from the environment to cigarette smoking. Hence, throughout U.S. history, policymakers have had to constantly balance this conflict between the common good and the right of the individual to choose freely. This has resulted in what will be referred to as the "ethics of sacrifice" versus the "ethics of tolerance."

Ethics of Sacrifice

When sacrifice as a moral concept is used to advance the merits of a particular issue, policymakers must be able to persuade the public to give up some benefit or "right" in order to achieve a noble goal or end. While it can easily be invoked by religious leaders, it can also be employed by political leaders in times of great national crisis, such as during World Wars I and II. In terms of traditional ethical or moral categories, sacrifice is teleological, that is, goal- or end-oriented. The goal is the "good" of society, and the "goodness" of any action is measured by what it contributes to maintaining the good of society.

In terms of public policy, the "good end" is a harmonious society. Traditionally, this ethic has been invoked by those wanting to maintain a certain social structure that they deem to be desirable whatever the cost. Witness the concern over "family values." While some might associate this type of ethical reasoning with conservative policymakers, actually both conservative and liberal thinkers have used it to justify their stance on major public-policy issues. "Liberal" politicians such as John F. Kennedy certainly invoked the ethics of sacrifice with his famous phrase: "Ask not what your country can do for you; ask what you can do for your country." In essence, those who subscribe to the ethics of sacrifice are asking the public to sublimate the good of the individual to the good of all.

An interesting example of such a public-policy issue was Prohibition. Supporters of a total ban on alcohol argued that alcohol abuse contributed to the disintegration of many families throughout the United States. So to preserve the sanctity of the family, a person's right to drink alcohol had to be sacrificed. Society could no longer condone the waste of human life attributed to alcohol. In the eyes of prohibitionists, the "good" achieved through the establishment of Prohibition more than outweighed the individual's right to drink alcohol. It soon became apparent, however, that the majority of the public was not willing to sacrifice its alcoholic beverages. Prohibition was repealed, and this experiment of enforced sacrifice was abandoned.

In the extreme, those who invoke the ethics of sacrifice can be accused of employing the motto, "The ends justify the means." The individual's ability to decide what is best for himself needs to be subservient to the needs of the state. The good of the state overrides the rights and needs of the individual. This is certainly the ethic under which the military and religious orders operate. However, when applied to a society with many diverse parts, it can have disastrous consequences. One need only recall the communist experience throughout the past eight decades. Yet it is an ethic that calls forth what some would maintain is the noblest of human characteristics, the ability to give of oneself even if that giving is detrimental to the individual.

Ethics of Tolerance

One of the first virtues that every American schoolchild is taught is tolerance. To escape religious persecution in England, the Quakers settled in Pennsylvania and are known for permitting others there to practice their own religious beliefs. In founding Maryland, Lord Baltimore established freedom of religion, especially for persecuted English

Catholics, although this tolerance would be tested frequently throughout the colonial period. The Pilgrims who settled in Massachusetts were also trying to escape religious persecution; however, tolerance was not a Puritan virtue, as Roger Williams quickly found out when he was forced to flee Massachusetts and establish Rhode Island. Although America has had its difficulties during its history, one of its hallmarks, in comparison to most countries, has been its tolerance for different religions as well as nationalities.

Tolerance implies that no person has to sacrifice his basic freedoms to achieve some goal of public welfare. Society cannot "tolerate" the abandonment of any individual even if it must incur a heavy cost to "save" him from activities that are harmful to him. Tolerance also requires society to tolerate the "right" of the individual to perform actions that might well be destructive to society as long as that right to perform those activities is guaranteed by law. Traditionally, the ethics of tolerance would fall into the deontological mode of thinking, that is, the means used to achieve a goal are more important than the goal itself.

A recent example of where the ethics of tolerance has so far prevailed in the public-policy forum is the second-hand smoke issue. Opponents of cigarette smoking, who had relied on the ethics of sacrifice, now maintain that the right to smoke cigarettes cannot be tolerated because it has been proven to have a negative impact on non-smokers. Meanwhile, American society has deemed gambling an activity that is "victimless," and therefore the "right" to gamble has been upheld.

The ethics of tolerance is based upon a noble American value and experiment, never to view a citizen as a means to achieve an end. Government exists to protect the individual's rights and must not coerce him to relinquish a right even for a good purpose. It is a value that in many ways is necessary in a country of immigrants. These immigrants had to be tolerated and protected to promote diversity. But like most values, it also has its downside. At its worst, tolerance can promote a rather narrow, selfish focus on the individual with little regard for how individuals need to relate to one another to live in society. For this glorification of the individual makes it quite difficult for society to challenge the individual to make the sacrifices necessary for everyone to live in harmony.

The Need for Moral Balance

In analyzing why the issue of casino gambling has evolved so differently from the issue of cigarette smoking over the past thirty years, it appears that the rights of individuals (ethics of tolerance) have triumphed over the good of a society (ethics of sacrifice). With the triumph of the ethics of tolerance it appears that the new categorical imperative is: "You have the right to perform any action as long as that action does not interfere with the rights of others."

This triumph of the ethics of tolerance does not preclude the ethics of sacrifice from either playing a significant role in the current public-policy process or triumphing again in the future. But it does indicate the current trend of settling public-policy issues in favor of those who can generate their arguments based on the ethics of tolerance.

The continuing support that policymakers give to gaming activities confirms the present cultural tendency to withdraw from public accountability into a cocoon of privacy. This preoccupation with the self (or privacy) poses some real challenges to the whole system of values and obligations that have historically been the basis of community and our cherished institutions such as the family.

Letting people be "free" to do what they want as long as they do not hurt others is hardly the type of ethic required when our society seems to be so desperately in need of a unifying communitarian spirit. Of course, this is not a call to subjugate the "self" or individual freedom totally under the banner of communitarian or institutional demand. But certainly the current rise in gaming activity points out a real need for an ethic for refereeing between the legitimate needs of society and the yearning of the self.

Whether the spread and acceptance of gambling as a form of entertainment will continue at their present pace depends on the continued acceptance of an ethic that places an absolute premium on the expression of the self over any claim for communitarian or institutional need. It is this glorification of the self that makes gambling not only a possibility but a necessity.

While the rise of gaming has many implications for America, as well as many other countries, perhaps the greatest challenge it presents is to restore a balance between the concerns of those who support the ethics of tolerance and those who support the ethics of sacrifice. The ability of a society to balance these moral viewpoints is the hallmark of a healthy and vibrant democratic system that the world desperately needs as it enters the twenty-first century.

Taking Chances on Casinos

Kevin Heubusch

Despite Americans' mixed feelings about gambling, increasing numbers of them are visiting casinos, reports *American Demographics* assistant editor Kevin Heubusch. The recent proliferation of casinos throughout the nation has made Americans more comfortable with the idea of gambling, Heubusch maintains. To capitalize on this increased openness to gambling, he writes, casinos now draw more customers by featuring new games, elaborate entertainment, and convenience—complete with carnival rides, Hollywood sets, video arcades, and child care.

A siren sounds, lights flash, and a woman shrieks. A crowd gathers. There's been a killing. On a casino riverboat gliding down the Des Plaines River in Illinois, a woman has just won $5,000 from a 50-cent slot machine.

The rapid rise of legalized public gaming in the U.S. has created a rush to attract wagers, a scramble to collect taxes, and worries about possible resulting social ills. But there is nothing complicated here on board Harrah's *Southern Star* in Joliet, Illinois. A slot attendant hurries up to congratulate the stunned player, shut off the siren, and write out a jackpot request slip.

Recreational gambling is moving into the mainstream. Fifty-six percent of Americans gambled at least once in 1996, according to Roper Starch Worldwide Inc. of New York City. Casino games and state-run lotteries were the most popular gambles. For the majority who anted up, the wager was not dramatic. Six in ten lottery players report spending less than $10 per month on tickets in 1996, according to a CNN/*USA Today* survey by Gallup. But $1 scratch tickets and quarter slot tokens add up. Americans spent $44.4 billion on wagers in 1995, according to research by Christiansen/Cummings Associates, Inc. in *International Gaming & Wagering Business* magazine. That's more than three times the combined amount they spent on box-office movies and theme parks.

"Gambling is play in the simplest sense," says Bill Eadington, director of the Institute for the Study of Gambling and Commercial Gaming at the University of Nevada, Reno. "But it deals with two funda-

Reprinted from Kevin Heubusch, "Taking Chances on Casinos," *American Demographics*, May 1997, with permission. ©1997, Cowles Business Media, Ithaca, New York.

mentals: chance and money." Those are no trifling matters.

Americans respect chance. Fifty-six percent say that chance plays a somewhat to very important role in how a person's life works out, according to the General Social Survey conducted by the Chicago-based National Opinion Research Center. At the same time, two-thirds agree that hard work is the most important reason why people get ahead. Mix these beliefs with the Protestant work ethic, stories of compulsive gamblers who win or lose everything, and a national history of successful wagers from western mining boomtowns to Wall Street, and simple play becomes complex controversy.

Changing Attitudes

U.S. attitudes toward gambling have never been simple. Our folklore is full of romantic risk-takers and errant gambling husbands. Lotteries, although popular in the 1800s, were banned in all states by the turn of the 20th century because of widespread fraud and corruption. In many people's minds, organized gambling became synonymous with organized crime.

But two changes in recent decades have improved the American public opinion of gambling. In 1964, New Hampshire introduced the first 20th-century public lottery in the U.S. Although lotteries may be controversial on ethical grounds, says Eadington, the New Hampshire lottery provided an example of "sanitized" gambling. Thirty-six states now sponsor lotteries. Casinos have capitalized on this public acceptance, cultivating an image as friendly and fun as a cross between a theme park and a shopping mall.

The second change follows on the first: increased exposure. Gambling has become less threatening to many people as gambling opportunities become more common. And gambling opportunities are becoming very common. A state lottery ticket and quart of milk can be purchased at the same convenience-store counter. Casino games, restricted to the Nevada desert prior to 1976, are available in downtown casinos, on riverboats, and on Indian reservations in 24 states.

The race to take your bet has already moved outside of casinos. Adults with a credit card and Internet access can wager on virtual casino games ("Can you think of anything better than your own private casino waiting for you at any time?" boasts one home page). Eight miles above the earth, airline passengers on some international non-U.S. flights can play seat-back video casino games for money.

Regardless of game, sponsor, or locale, a solid segment of the public still believes gambling is wrong. Twenty-seven percent of adults say gambling is immoral, according to a 1996 Gallup Organization poll, although the share is down from 32 percent in 1992. Older adults and Protestants are most likely to disapprove of gambling.

Gamblers, not surprisingly, have the most positive opinions about gambling. But nongamblers are not necessarily more likely than average to consider gambling immoral. Among people who did not gamble in the previous year, 25 percent say they didn't gamble because of moral or religious objections, according to a 1993 Roper survey. The reasons most people give for not gambling are that they don't want to spend the money (35 percent) and they don't have the money to spend (33 percent).

Social Qualms vs. Economic Boosts

Although most Americans do not consider gambling immoral, many Americans are not at ease with its potential effect on their neighbors and neighborhoods. Forty-two percent of Americans agree that allowing more casinos to open "threatens our values," according to a 1996 Roper survey. Forty-one percent say that casinos disrupt the quality of life in the surrounding area.

Two-thirds of people agree that legalized gambling encourages the people who can least afford it to squander their money, according to the Gallup Organization. Sixty-one percent say that legalized gambling can make a compulsive gambler out of a person who would never gamble illegally.

But gambling does not loom as a public threat, even if it does have a significant reputation of bilking the poor and addicting the lawful. Among major social problems such as drug addiction or drunk driving, Americans rate gambling pretty low—below prostitution and above social drinking, according to Roper.

Proponents claim that casinos are just like any other business that meets a demand, and nearly half of Americans agree. But a different argument often wins casinos a license. Said simply: taxes. Many localities that face diminishing state and federal money, rising property taxes, and sluggish economies eye casinos as welcome sources of revenue. Ethical arguments are hard to pin down, but substituting a raise in property taxes with a special casino tax is a solid argument. States and localities collected an estimated $16 billion in gambling privilege taxes in 1995. Nevada raises 40 percent of its state tax revenue from Las Vegas casinos.

Las Vegas would likely evaporate if the resort casino industry moved or closed down. The rest of the nation is less dependent on gaming revenue, but it does contribute significantly to local budgets in many places. Other towns with newly licensed casinos are still waiting for the flood of tourists and tax money.

Most Americans have a positive attitude toward gambling's impact on local economies. Nearly two-thirds of adults say that casinos create a lot of jobs and tax revenues, according to Roper. Sixty-five percent agree that state-sponsored gambling stimulates local economies, and half say it provides revenue for education and senior citizens. A pragmatic 62 percent of respondents say that people will gamble whether gambling is legal or not, so the state may as well get a piece of the action, according to a 1996 Gallup/CNBC poll.

Who Gambles?

Ethics and economics aside, just over half of Americans gambled at least once in 1995 (56 percent). The most popular gamble was on a state lottery (45 percent), followed by a visit to a casino (20 percent). The overall share of risk-takers is virtually the same as in 1988, when 54 percent of adults made a wager. The big change in recent years is in where people are gambling.

Bingo parlors and race tracks saw little change in attendance between 1988 and 1996, according to Roper. The share of people who reported playing lotteries grew by only 3 percentage points over the same eight years; most state lotteries were already in place by the late 1980s. But the share of adults who visited a casino in the previous year rose from 12 to 20 percent between 1988 and 1996. This increase parallels the boom in casino growth that began in 1988–89. In relatively short order, limited casino gaming was approved in South Dakota, Iowa, Illinois, Mississippi, Missouri, and on Indian reservations nationwide. Casinos now account for 41 percent of all money spent on wagers, according to Christiansen/Cummings.

U.S. casinos have not tapped a hidden Monte Carlo crowd of James Bonds. They have reached the mainstream. The most striking demographic feature of modern casino gamblers is their lack of striking demographic features.

Gambling of all types typically increases with income, usually indicating greater discretionary income and increased accessibility to gambling venues. Participation in the most accessible games, such as bingo and lotteries, is highest for those with middle incomes, while casino gambling peaks with the highest incomes and levels of education. Among those with incomes below $15,000 in 1996, only one in ten visited a casino in the previous year. For those with incomes of $75,000 or more, the share was one in three. Casino gamblers exhibit other traits related to high income. They are more likely than average to have a college degree, are more likely than average to have white-collar jobs, and are likely to be in the peak earning years of 45 to 54.

The typical casino visitor may have a higher-than-average income, but he or she is not adverse to adding to it. Winning money is the most important reason why people say they visit a casino. Three in four casino patrons say they go primarily to win "a really large amount of money," according to a Roper survey. Entertainment and recreation follow money, cited as an important reason for 57 percent of patrons.

Casinos attempt to balance these two customer expectations in advertising and on the casino floor. Clearly, casinos and patrons are somewhat at odds about the extent to which "really large amounts" of money can pass from the casino to the patron. Casinos may advertise the "loosest" slots, but more importantly, they promise unlimited entertainment.

Selling the Experience

The influx of new casino gamblers has changed the nature of casino business. The "traditional" blackjack player hedged against the house odds. But the new casino patron is more likely to think in terms of bargains. Fifty-seven percent of adults who'd been to a casino in the year before Roper interviewed them in 1993 said that "relatively cheap" entertainment was an important reason for going, up from 51 percent in 1988.

New casino patrons are not likely to be high rollers, and casino gaming profits increasingly depend on "churn"—cycling through a larger number of smaller bets. Quick service and convenience are also important to recent casino gamblers. More than one-third say they visited a casino because casino gambling doesn't take much time. A look at the newest casinos on the Vegas strip and elsewhere illustrates how the battle for the mainstream gambler is changing the industry.

Las Vegas has never been demure, but neon lights and showgirls are no longer enough to draw customers. The city's newest casino, New York–New York Hotel & Casino, is a collision of downtown Manhattan and Walt Disney World at the south end of the Las Vegas strip. It features 12 Manhattan skyscrapers at one-third scale, a Coney Island–style roller coaster, a 100-yard-long Brooklyn Bridge, and a 150-foot Statue of Liberty, all of which house 84,000 square feet of casino space. New York–New York cost MGM Grand, Inc. and Primadonna Resorts, Inc. an estimated $460 million to construct. The price tag includes a bumper-car arena with model Checker cabs, laser-tag street fighting, and a lighted ball that drops every midnight outside the "Times Square" piano bar.

Further up the strip, the $550 million Stratosphere Hotel & Casino has the tallest free-standing observation tower in the U.S. (1,149 feet). Stratosphere Corporation went straight to Hollywood to hire its advertising firm. Cimarron/Bacon/O'Brien (CBO) Communications is a division of CBO whose clientele include Twentieth Century Fox, Disney Home Video, and Toyota Motor Sales. Prior to the Stratosphere campaign, CBO created movie trailers for *Terminator 2* and *Die Hard with a Vengeance*.

Another casino operator, Hollywood Casino Corporation, makes the casino-Hollywood connection complete. Using movie props such as an elephant from the movie *Operation Dumbo Drop*, the Tunica, Mississippi, casino offers Adventure Slots. The complete theme casino offers an experience akin to playing slot machines in the middle of *Raiders of the Lost Ark*. Visitors to the casino are greeted by a talking stone idol, a runaway mining cart that spills souvenir tokens, and a wrecked airplane in a tree with a skeleton hanging from the cockpit.

Every day is an adventure in new casinos, but special events don't pass unnoticed, either. Those tired of Christmas in Connecticut may want to try Christmas in Las Vegas or Hanukkah according to Hoyles.

[Edmond Hoyle authored a widely used rule book for games.] During the 1996 holiday season, Las Vegas boasted an outdoor skating rink (no mean feat in the middle of Nevada), twice-daily toy-soldier parades, and according to press releases, "the tallest menorah in Nevada."

But spectacle is only the start of casino marketing in the 1990s. Casinos intent on serving mainstream gamblers must meet them halfway. That's why the Stratosphere features state-of-the-art Super Tush 2000 seats. Many casinos include smoke-free gaming parlors. In St. Louis, The President Casino offers a frequent-players club where gamblers can earn discounted or complimentary meals and merchandise.

Station Casino Kansas City is making a bold play for the least-traditional casino patron: couples with children. The fourth-largest casino in the country is clearly family-friendly, offering a video arcade operated by Sega GameWorks, child care, quick-service food outlets, and an 18-screen cinema. This is also a young adult's casino that serves microbrew beers and Starbucks coffee. It's significant that another new casino—the Niagara Casino in Windsor, Canada—is housed in a former shopping mall.

Slots Crank Up the Pace

Casinos are doing more to broaden their appeal than just turning up the volume on their decor and non-gaming entertainment. The games themselves are changing. First-time visitors may have seen movie gamblers tackle the likes of craps, baccarat, and blackjack, but they're hesitant to make the plunge themselves. The novice who has been enticed by the elephant from *Operation Dumbo Drop* is unlikely to pick up the dice at a craps table and face the boxman, stickman, two dealers, and a half dozen bettors wagering the pass line on the come-out roll.

As a result, casinos are turning to faster, simpler, small-wager games. Slot machines are the most popular. Gamblers favor slots because they are easy to understand, fast-paced, and feature higher jackpots than traditional table games. Atlantic City originally allowed casinos to devote no more than 30 percent of their space to slots. The limit has been raised to 90 percent. Slots accounted for $10.8 billion in gross casino revenue in 1995—twice that of table games (not including revenues from non-casino venues and Indian casinos). Las Vegas alone houses nearly 165,000 slot machines. That's enough for almost one in nine Nevadans.

Slots are a game without strategy, a significant departure from card and dice games where players can play the odds to curb the house advantage and maximize their winnings. As James F. Smith of Penn State, Abington-Ogontz campus, writes: "One cannot play a . . . slot machine well; one can only play more. . . ."

The more people play, the more casinos make. Casinos increased slots 10 percent in 1995 and realized a 17 percent slot profit, according to Christiansen/Cummings. This has been a calculated move in more ways than one; casinos can program the machine's win rate. This doesn't mean slots are a losing gamble, however. Many casinos base their draw on "loose" slots—ones that pay back at a "better" rate. But as gambling writer Frank Scoblete says, the only way to really beat a slot machine is with a sledge hammer.

Some manufacturers of slot machines are upping the entertainment value by becoming more elaborate. A dot-matrix animated pig entertains the player in Piggy Bankin' produced by Williams (WMS) Gaming, Inc. When the piggy bank is full of coins, the player receives a bonus. Acres Gaming developed Hurricane Zone—a bank of slots below a 35-foot-long fiberglass cloud. When thunder and lightning strike each quarter hour, the payoff increases on the machines below.

With an eye toward an upcoming generation of casino gamblers, Casino Data Systems is developing a slot game called Gold Fever. The slot features an 18-minute movie that provides additional entertainment unrelated to the slot action. When players hit a special gold nugget in the course of slot action, the film changes to a ride down a gold mine shaft for a bonus prize. The company is also developing computer-animated slots that make a more direct link between video games and gambling devices. It doesn't have just the Nintendo generation in mind, either. The company thinks baby boomers want more entertainment value for their token.

Older slot players can be disenchanted with new machines, though. The manufacturer that dominates the market is paying attention to these mature customers. International Game Technology chairman Chuck Mathewson says his company has plenty of new technology, but will not rush it onto the casino floor before players are receptive to new slot games. Hans Kloss, president and COO of Bally Gaming International, Inc., says he doubts that slot gamblers want to play "in a kids' arcade."

Bye Bye, Blackjack?

The increase in slot machines has meant a decrease in table games, if only because of the finite space in a casino. But table games, predicted by some to go the way of the dinosaur several years ago, have not been swept aside yet. In fact, Dave Knapp, who oversees new games at Harrah's Las Vegas, confidently says that traditional casino games are here to stay. Knapp believes that younger players will graduate to table games such as craps or roulette exactly because these games offer a new experience. Harrah's Las Vegas does not tailor new table games to a player's generation, but to the player's level of experience. Because new players may be too intimidated to sit down at a blackjack or poker table, Knapp offers games that are easy to learn and simple to play.

Thus, gamblers at Harrah's Las Vegas can play Casino War. The house deals a card to each player and to itself. If a player has a higher card than the house, the player wins. The friendliest feature in a game such as this, Knapp says, is that the player can't make a mistake. The novice gambler needn't worry that a bad play on his or her part will negatively affect the hands of other players. "You get that sometimes," Knapp says of more complex games. "A table will groan if one player makes a bad play."

Getting players to sit down at a table also introduces them to the sociability and excitement of group games, says Knapp. Harrah's offers Party Pits to entice younger crowds. These are separate table areas where the action is a little more casual. Dealers are less formal, and the music is rock and roll.

Casinos want to bring in new customers, but they don't want to risk alienating their experienced patrons. Some new games are variations of traditional card games, altered to increase the pace and heighten the jackpot. For example, Spanish 21 removes cards from the deck and adds side bets and wild cards to traditional blackjack.

Increasing Cost and Competition

As the *Southern Star* docks at the end of its Illinois river cruise, a large crowd files off and another large crowd waits to board. Despite the crowds, the stakes are high for casinos. An average slot machine costs $5,000 to $6,000, and the new Station Casino Kansas City opened its doors boasting 3,000 of them. Talking stone idols, Super Tush 2000 seats, and Hollywood advertising firms are also not inexpensive, nor simple to finance. In January 1997, nine months after opening its doors, the Stratosphere in Las Vegas filed for bankruptcy protection. Days before, Donald Trump had sold a 51 percent interest in his Trump Castle in Atlantic City to raise cash for expansion. While these dramas unfolded, the Hilton Hotels Corp. initiated a $10.5 billion bid to become the largest hotel and casino operator in the world by taking over International Telephone and Telegraph (ITT) Corp. ITT owns Caesars casinos and Sheraton Hotels.

Increasing competition means declining market share. At the same time that casino owners are building bigger and brighter to keep market share, others are seeking to consolidate the market. Less than eight years after the current casino boom began, many in the industry are warning against overbuilding, especially in hotels. As one analyst puts it, Las Vegas won't know how many hotel rooms are too many until it builds the hotel that doesn't fill.

Cities that depend on gambling taxes are also obsessed with maintaining their casinos' market share. If casinos become widespread enough to saturate local markets, local governments can expect to draw fewer tourist dollars and tax revenues from residents of other places. Cities must also rely on casinos to keep the customers coming back. If the public's enthusiasm for casino gaming peaks as it has seemingly done with maturing state lotteries, even the locals won't be gambling as much.

Controversy over casinos remains high. Most Americans seem to consider gambling a permissible indulgence. Yet many remain unconvinced that casinos can solve more problems than they create. Despite all the familiar economic promises, a legislative measure that would have allowed private casinos outside of Indian reservations in New York State failed in 1997.

States and cities contemplating the legalization of casino gambling will be keeping a close eye on those who are now trying to get their piece of the Vegas action. If casinos can responsibly handle concerns about problem gambling and deliver on the promise of local prosperity, public opinion could very well remain on the side of Lady Luck. But it's not a sure bet.

THE JOY OF GAMBLING

David Spanier

In David Spanier's opinion, the pleasure of playful, active risk-taking is the true appeal of gambling. He describes the allure of various forms of betting, including the "long-shot gamble" of state lotteries, which allow players to dream about sudden fortune, and the "short-term thrill" of casino games, which offer players intense emotional and physical excitement. Although Spanier maintains that gambling can provide an exhilarating reprieve from day-to-day life, he does not believe that the rewards of gambling always outweigh its pitfalls. Gambling, he concludes, should be controlled and regulated to curb compulsive behavior and to maintain the economic stability of communities impacted by gambling revenues. Spanier, a London journalist, is the author of *Welcome to the Pleasuredome: Inside Las Vegas.*

> The action is everything, more consuming than sex, more immediate than politics, more important always than the acquisition of money.   —Joan Didion, *The White Album*

What if you met a man in a bar this evening, after you quit work for the day, and he said (as people sometimes do), "Hey, let's toss a coin for a dollar, heads or tails."

"Right here in front of everybody?"

"Why not!"

"Okay," you might say, if you were in that sort of mood. "Let's go for it!"

But then the man adds: "Just one little thing about this toss I want to explain before we start. When I win, you lose your dollar. When you win, I'll pay you only 99 cents."

It's not all that different, is it, one penny on the toss? But you would be out of your mind to take on such a proposition, wouldn't you? Especially if your spouse or, worse, your employer, happened to be watching. You would be marked down as an idiot if you couldn't handle your money any better. A dollar to 99 cents. Why do it? It makes no sense.

But that is exactly what all of us do when we gamble, when we cross the threshold between workaday life and the fantasy realm of a

Reprinted from David Spanier, "The Joy of Gambling," *Wilson Quarterly*, Autumn 1995, by permission of the author.

casino. In fact, if the house gets only one percent of an edge or advantage (as in certain bets at dice), gamblers consider it a good bet. If they can get even money, one for one on their stake, they think it's great value, as in certain bets at dice.

The Laws of Probability

I have a confession to make, right at the start. I am not a gambler. Not any more, that is. I have learned the hard way, as most of us do, that you cannot beat the laws of probability.

On my first visit to Las Vegas, as a freshman on vacation from Cambridge University, I came prepared with a system for roulette. My idea was to wait for a series of reds or blacks to come up, six in a row, and then start betting on the other color, doubling up after each losing spin until I hit a winner. So after six reds, say, I would start betting black: $1, then $2, $4, $8, $16, $32, $64, $128. For the system to lose, the same color would have to come up 15 times in a row, which seemed highly unlikely. My only anxiety, as I recall, was that the initial run of six consecutive reds or blacks would take such a long time to appear that I might get bored waiting.

I need not have worried. After a couple of hours logging the wheel, I was ready to launch my system. The first spin went down, the next spin went down, and the next, and the next, with terrifying speed, as red kept repeating. Suddenly, like a flash of light striking a philosopher, the realization penetrated my fevered brow. This particular roulette wheel did not give a damn about me and my pathetic hopes of fortune. It was oblivious to the fact that I had traveled 7,000 miles across an ocean and most of a continent to test my luck. If I was to follow my system, I had to bet $256 on the next spin. I also had six weeks of summer vacation to pay for. The croupier was eyeing my precarious tower of chips like an explosives expert about to dynamite a building. I pulled back—just in time.

Nearly everyone makes this mistake in gambling, which is to confuse the short-term outcome with long-term probability. On every individual spin, the probability of red or black is the same, 50:50. And over a million spins, reds and blacks will virtually even out (ignoring zeros). But within that series, there will be many short-term fluctuations on either side. Fourteen reds in a row is no big deal.

Risk Taking in Its Purest Form

It is good to learn this lesson young. When I go to Las Vegas now, I don't even *see* the slot machines. I feel almost guilty—considering the immense and multifarious efforts the casinos make to tempt the visitor to gamble—that I do not spend a dime on casino games. My passion lies elsewhere. I play poker, a game of skill, albeit with a big gambling element in it. What I like is the ambience of gambling, particularly casino gambling, with its day-into-night and night-into-day sense of anything-goes-and-here-it-comes release from the conventions of ordinary life.

Everyone takes chances, every day, although people do not consciously classify the process as gambling. Every time you drive, every time you buckle up in an airplane seat, one might say every time you cross the road, the risk is there. These are unavoidable risks in the modern world and, for most people, so habitual as not to be worth worrying about. *Che sera sera.* These days, there is danger in riding the subway, danger in visiting New York's World Trade Center, danger even in visiting a government building in Oklahoma City, let alone in traveling abroad.

Other sorts of risks, such as those inherent in active sports such as skiing, mountaineering, horseback riding, sailing, and football, are more easily avoided. The pleasure of doing it is what gets people involved. That pleasure far outweighs any vestigial concern about something going wrong. Besides, regardless of the sport, everyone involved has had at least a degree of initial training to prepare himself or herself and to guard against accidents. The odds of coming through safely are tilted well in your favor.

Even in matters of investment, such as taking out a life insurance policy, which means, in effect, betting on your own longevity, the gamble is a studied risk, founded on actuarial tables and the prudent desire to protect your family. The insurance company, working on the past record of hundreds of thousands of instances, calculates the probability of a particular misfortune befalling the applicant, and sets its premium accordingly, adding a healthy margin to cover operating costs and allow for a profit.

The insurance companies are not really gambling themselves, because they are operating on the basis of statistics that virtually guarantee them a positive return. Yes, but then we remember [the failure of the insurers] Lloyd's of London. Even the best-regulated risks sometimes come unstuck. I think it was James Thurber who observed: "There is no safety in numbers; there is no safety anywhere."

Casino gambling is risk taking in its purest form. The participants willingly and deliberately get involved, knowing the chances are not in their favor. No one has to do it. All players are aware that the odds are against them. The odds are set out in all the books, even in government reports on gambling. The question is: why do people still do it?

The True Appeal of Gambling

It may seem a paradox to insist that money is not what gambling is about. Of course, money is the essence of gambling and the way you keep score. Games of chance without money involved simply do not work. And you cannot gamble in a casino without money. Money is the fuel of gambling; it drives it, as gasoline powers a car. But the pleasure of driving a car is not about gas. It's about speed, style, movement. Gas is only what makes the car run. In that sense, the real motives behind gambling are to be sought elsewhere.

Play, the enjoyment of play, is a part of human nature. It is an instinct as old as the sex drive, as powerful as hunger and thirst, as basic to the human condition as survival. Gambling is a heightened form of play. That is why so many people like gambling, and spend so much money on it, not just all over the United States now that the brakes are off but in virtually all societies in the modern world.

The appeal of gambling, to my mind, is in the *action*. The phrase "where the action is" derives from Damon Runyon's story, "The Idyll of Miss Sarah Brown" (1947), which celebrates the exploits of gambler Sky Masterson. The immortal Sky Masterson got his name, you may remember, because he liked to bet so high, on any proposition whatever, that he would bet all he had. "The Sky is strictly a player. . . . As far as The Sky is concerned, money is just something for him to play with and the dollars may as well be doughnuts as far as value goes with him."

Action expresses, in a word, the whole gambling experience. It means playing with chance, taking a challenge, the excitement of living in top gear. In gambling, this is the payoff. In our routinized urban lives, most of us are cogs in the wheel of work, taxes, and social and family obligations. Gambling offers a fast way out. On the green baize, or at the track, or at a lottery terminal, the player can give self-indulgence a whirl, briefly cast responsibility aside, and fantasize about a brighter, richer, easier life. It is not, in reality, going to work out like that. But some people do win, don't they? In lotteries, almost unimaginable sums of money.

Gambling's Payoffs

Here it is useful to distinguish different forms of gambling by the payoffs they offer: long-term versus short-term; degrees of social gratification; profit and loss. Each kind of gamble offers its own appeal.

First, the long-shot gamble, as in lotteries. In terms of odds, of many millions to one against winning, lotteries are a bad gamble. Their appeal, which certainly elicits a deep response across a huge swath of the population, lies in the prospect of acquiring superstar wealth, as if the finger of fate were suddenly to reach out and touch one lucky person. All of this can be purchased for a very small price. For a period before the draw—it may be just a few minutes, or may last for days—people can daydream about what they would do with the money. And why not? It is a harmless enough little dream, which can lighten dull lives. Lottery players know that only one winner will make it big. What their purchase of a ticket gives them is a little spoonful of hope, which, like honey, is pleasing while it lasts.

Experience shows that lotteries tend to exploit low-income sectors of the population. Besides being least able to afford this kind of spending, which is of course an indirect form of taxation, such people tend to be most vulnerable to the lottery promoters' blandishments. Indeed, what may be most troubling about lotteries are slogans like "Your way out of the ghetto" and other enticements used by state agencies to attract bettors.

A great deal of gambling, at the popular level, is geared to a short-term thrill. This is what casinos offer. Unlike with lotteries, the odds seem within reach. Casino gamblers look down on lotteries because the odds are too long to offer a practical expectation of gain, whereas slot machines, dice, blackjack, and roulette can provide an immediate return. At a fast-moving game of roulette, there may be more than 60 coups an hour: a slot machine, without the intermediary of a dealer or croupier, or any need for know-how on the part of the player, offers perhaps five or six coups per minute. With a slot machine, the thrill of the action as the gambler inserts the coins, pulls the handle, or presses the buttons, is almost continuous—as long as the money lasts. The American people have become so enamored of slots that they now account for about 65 percent of casino gambling.

It should be noted, in passing, that there is no skill involved in casino games (with the single exception of blackjack). What gamblers get is speed and intensity of action, plus the chance of hitting a winning streak that can lead to a big win, the win that will salve all their previous losses. At roulette, the queen of casino games, hitting the right number pays 35 to 1. Never mind that the edge against the player on the double-zero game is an iniquitous 5.26 percent, compared with only 2.7 percent on the single-zero European game. If luck, i.e. short-term fluctuation, runs your way, you can break the bank or at least win a small fortune. (What is the sure-fire way to make a small fortune in a casino? Answer: start off with a large fortune.)

Getting the Adrenaline Going

The gambling games offered by casinos act like a drug. It's part physical, part psychological, highs and lows, over and over, in rapid succession. These fluctuations of loss and gain, the glint of light and action, awareness of other people gambling, the sense underneath it all of playing with risk, of living on the edge of danger, are exciting. This is what the expression "getting the adrenaline going" means. The physical sensation—dryness in the throat, sweaty palms, butterflies in the stomach, the feeling of every nerve on full alert—is, for many people, highly pleasurable. Some psychologists have suggested a parallel between gambling and sexual excitement: build-up, climax, release of tension, repeated over and over. There is no need to press the analogy too far to make the point that gambling carries a strong emotional charge.

To increase the sense of indulgence, of fantasy, of losing hold of reality, casinos create an ambience far removed from the surround of ordinary life. No clocks. No daylight. Seductive lighting. Flashes of surreal color. The whir of the slots. The beat of music, pulsing under the noise of greetings, shouts, ringing jackpots, whoops from the winners. Drinks on the house—"Keep 'em coming, baby!"—and on every side, the half-open sexual turn-on of cutey-pie dealers in party dress or cowboy gear. What a heady, glamorous mix! How can anyone long resist it? All of it designed to disorient the gamblers and keep them playing. The whole operation driven—this is most important—by easy credit. "Another 2,000, Mr. Ashuro, just sign this slip, sir."

The social component of gambling, varying from game to game, finds its most extreme expression in baccarat. The baccarat pit is usually separated from the casino floor by a rail; bystanders can admire or envy it, at a distance. The excitement of baccarat comes from the sheer size of the stakes, up to $250,000 a hand in the case of Australian tycoon Kerry Packer and a few other very rich men. Again, it is a game requiring no skill whatsoever. (Two sides, Bank and Player, each draw two cards with the option of a third card, to see who gets closer to a total of nine.) Baccarat caters to a select group of monied players who probably can afford more or less anything they want in material terms but who relish the challenge of high-stakes play, of taking on the house. The players know that each hand is the equivalent of, say, the price of a Cadillac, but the bets are treated simply as so many plastic chips.

What gives this kind of gambling its cachet, its style, is not just the high stakes but another dimension of the game, which might be termed "social pampering." Baccarat provides a handful of top casinos—there is a pecking order among casinos as well—with the cream of their revenue. The managers of these casinos will do anything and everything to attract the high rollers: not merely the routine "comps" (complimentary services) of a free flight and private suite accorded all big gamblers, but the kind of personal attention (such as a favorite chef on call 24 hours a day) designed to gratify a particular customer's every whim. Such high pampering is not readily obtainable in ordinary life, even to the rich. (Girls? Perish the thought! Las Vegas casinos claim they would never risk their gaming licenses for petty prostitution.)

Casino staffs include a particular category of employee called a "host" whose role is to take care of high rollers: the host and the guest each understand that their relationship, cordial as it may be, is based on a false premise—namely the narrow 1.2 percent house edge on baccarat which, cumulatively, is immensely profitable to the casino. But both sides conspire to accept the relationship at face value. (Sometimes the players win a million or two, but so long as they keep coming back, the casino isn't worried.)

Horse Racing

The social aspect of gambling comes out most clearly in horse racing. The race track offers a quite different kind of gamble from casino play.

For one thing, racing has a public image: people attend race tracks in large numbers, and they read about racing in the papers. The sport can be enjoyed for its own sake. Racing brings together a wide-ranging fraternity of owners, trainers, jockeys, and other followers whose common link is their enthusiasm for the game. In England, this identity of interest runs from Queen Elizabeth herself all the way down to the cloth-capped punter at the street bookie.

More significantly, from the gambling point of view, horse racing (unlike most casino games) allows room for judgment. The bettor has lots of information to weigh: all the variables of running, timing, handicapping, etc. that comprise form. Horse-race players are notably studious, and the intervals set between races allow time to resolve the more or less insoluble equation of form, to pick a winner. This is a relatively measured form of betting, but being available almost every day, it still carries as much risk of becoming compulsive as any other form of gambling. It is satisfying to make your own judgment (especially if it proves right), but racing is still a gamble—much more so than games such as bridge or backgammon, in which a player's skill, in the shape of his or her own decisions, determines the result.

Professional Gambling

The element of skill finds its most complete expression in professional gambling. As the odds in gambling are, by definition, against the player, "professional gambling" is something of a misnomer. It connotes players who have managed to turn the odds in their favor. The only casino game in which this occurs is blackjack. Thanks to mathematician Edward Thorp's landmark book *Beat the Dealer* (1962), many thousands of players have learned "counting" (a way of keeping track of the cards in order to increase the stakes when the outcome appears favorable; casinos hate counters and do their best to bar them). "You have to be smart enough to understand the game and dumb enough to think it matters," comments Peter Griffin, author of another treatise on blackjack.

Professional card players certainly exist: poker players, who expect to win more than they lose, and follow no other occupation, work longer hours than many accountants. In the United States, they pay income tax on their earnings. Their edge comes from exploiting the weakness of less-skilled players. "Ain't only three things to gamblin'," according to W.C. "Puggy" Pearson, former world poker champion. "Knowin' the 60:40 end of a proposition, money management, and knowin' yourself." There is at the same time a camaraderie among groups of gamblers, whether they are card players or horse-race players (or stock market speculators), which gives their activity an added dimension of a sense of belonging beyond the activity itself.

The truly professional gamblers are the casinos themselves. "If you wanna make money in a casino, own one!" advises Steve Wynn, president of Mirage Resorts, Inc. As the most successful operator in the gaming industry, he has proved his point. The casinos, by gratifying the gambling instincts of the rest of us, are betting on a sure thing. The odds are always in their favor. And if they get the operation right (not as easy it looks, as competition gets tougher), they must win. It took Wall Street some time to grasp this essential truth and accept casino stocks as respectable, but they are now a popular—perhaps even blue-chip—investment.

The rise of privately and publicly sponsored legalized gambling has consequences that are double-edged in different ways for communities and individuals. And the irony is that while the individual pleasures and psychic rewards of gambling have been generally underappreciated, the social and economic benefits of legalized betting are generally overestimated.

The U.S. Gambling Spree

It was Atlantic City that launched the gambling spree across the United States, taking it well beyond the arid confines of Nevada. The first casino opened its doors on the Boardwalk in 1978. Atlantic City became a model for other jurisdictions eager to cash in, so they fondly imagined, on easy money. It was an unfortunate model, because, as anyone who has been there can vouch, Atlantic City is a dismal failure. Instead of being transformed into a new community, the old resort has remained essentially what it was, a glorified dump.

There are exceptions to the Atlantic City model. The most extraordinary, surreal even, eruption of gambling in America has occurred in an unlikely location: the green hills of Connecticut. Foxwoods, on the 2,000-acre reservation of the Mashantucket Pequot tribe, is now the most successful casino in the United States, indeed, in the English-speaking world. It plays host to 45,000 visitors a day. Its annual "drop" (money gambled) is more than $800 million, its total "win" (money held after paying out the winners, before expenses) around 20 percent of this sum. And all this since 1991. Foxwoods has brought thousands of new jobs to a region in decline. The collapse of the shipbuilding industry in New London, Connecticut, as the result of post–Cold War military cutbacks cost 6,000 jobs. Foxwoods has more than made up this total and has plans to add still more hotels and entertainment attractions.

The Need for Control

Yet many of the jurisdictions that are so confidently promoting gambling today will discover that the economic benefits are illusory. Even Foxwoods could some day see an end to the easy money as competition in the region rises. What tends to occur is a diversion, rather than a net growth of economic resources. Gambling is, after all, different from other leisure activities. It can so easily destroy people. It can encourage false hopes, undermine thrift, and lead to compulsive behavior. It must be prudently controlled. The risk now is that it may do some of these things to entire communities as well. Even those (such as myself) who appreciate the revivifying effects of a night at the casino or a day at the race track may care to shade their bets in the face of the gambling fever that now grips the United States.

CASINO WORKERS: HIGH LEVELS OF STRESS AND BURNOUT

Jon Nordheimer

In the following selection, Jon Nordheimer reports on his interviews with several Atlantic City casino workers about the stresses and frustrations of their jobs. Although casino workers are paid well, he maintains, they face unpredictable work hours, overexposure to loud noises and bright lights, boredom from repetitive activities, and little chance for advancement. According to Nordheimer, casino workers are often treated poorly by customers and by management; moreover, some card dealers become compulsive gamblers. Nordheimer is a *New York Times* journalist.

The night the high roller dropped dead and casino workers rolled his body beneath the craps table so the game could proceed was Vinnie Springer's confirmation of the relentlessness of the game.

"Even when the paramedics came to remove the body 15 minutes later, the dice kept rolling," said Mr. Springer, a tall, amiable 40-year-old man who has worked as a craps stick man and blackjack dealer at Atlantic City casinos for the last 10 years.

Mr. Springer is part of the elite of Atlantic City's work force, the men and women who work the casino tables, winning or losing millions of dollars for the house on each eight-hour shift.

A Demanding Workplace

It is high-pressure work, as stressful on a daily basis as being a big-city cop or an emergency room nurse, and signs of wear and tear on casino workers are becoming more pronounced.

"Behind the bright lights and the glamour are a lot of unhappy workers who earn white-collar pay for what are essentially blue-collar jobs," said Sandy Festa, an alcohol and drug counselor who also treats casino workers for a number of job-related complaints like depression and anxiety.

"They make too much money to leave, but they can't stand the thought of doing the same thing day after day for the rest of their lives," Ms. Festa said. "It's what is known in the trade as casino burnout."

Her husband, Elliott, who has been a blackjack and craps worker for 14 years, added, "You reach a point where you either take the job one day at a time or else quit and do something earning less money, but without all the stress."

Among the chief complaints are casino work shifts, which are shuffled as often as decks of cards in the round-the-clock operations. Working on weekends and holidays. Boredom in roles that require a degree of cleverness in counting but not much more. Little chance for promotion.

Add to that the constant audio and visual overload of a casino floor—glittering lights, the clatter of coins and ringing bells from slot machine payoffs, the stutter of roulette wheels and the whoop of joy or anguish from players—and the casino can be a very demanding workplace.

Casino officials say the complaints are similar to grievances that arise in any workplace about unsympathetic supervisors or slow advancement. What adds new wrinkles are the dynamics of gambling, said Michelle Perna, vice president of human resources for Merv Griffin's Resorts Casino Hotel.

"Our workers are paid well to make sure people have a good time," Ms. Perna said. "And that can be stressful if people are losing money."

High Pay and High Pressure

Many casino workers, Mr. Springer included, count themselves lucky to hold jobs that can pay $40,000 a year, mostly in pooled tips—though the average may be closer to $30,000—and that place them in the center of the action.

"Each day working in a casino is like New Year's Eve anywhere else," he said with a broad smile.

He rattled off the names of celebrities and sports stars he has met on the job.

His co-worker, Billy Sullivan, nodded in agreement. "Real good people who treat you right," said Mr. Sullivan, who was joining Mr. Springer for an after-work round of drinks, shortly before 5 A.M., in the Chelsea Pub, a half-block from the boardwalk and the bright lights of Atlantic City's 12 casino towers, which employ 50,000 workers.

But they also described venomous encounters with players who blamed them for their losses, as well as big shots who treated them like dirt.

They and other casino workers all recall high rollers who years ago were given the red carpet treatment everywhere they went and today are broke, scavenging through the payoff basins of slot machines for overlooked coins.

"They're all searching for that lucky streak that'll win back what they lost," said a woman who quit working as a croupier after three years to return to college. Like many other past and present casino workers, she spoke only on the condition of anonymity. "I may want my job back some day," she explains.

She said she left the casinos because job pressures were getting to her.

"My mother was a pit boss and it was her whole life," she said. "I couldn't take the constantly changing hours and constantly being caught between management and the customers. Everyone's watching your every move, including the surveillance cameras in the ceiling, and one mistake really puts the heat on you.

"If your table is losing unusual amounts of money, the pit bosses start sweating and watch you even more closely to see if you're trying to 'help out' a customer."

Moreover, she said, there were the "guard dogs" or "blue coats"— dealer parlance for the Casino Control Commission agents stationed on every casino floor to enforce state regulations—who, she said, could "nit-pick on every rule in the book."

She was also bothered, she said, by the antipathy of some gamblers for women dealers, especially at the craps tables, where superstition rules just about every decision of some players. "They think women are unlucky and they don't want you to touch the dice," she said.

Her worst moment: A high roller on a hot streak refused to leave the craps table to go to a rest room after hours of play, and he relieved himself under the table, sending her and other croupiers scattering. "He went on playing as though nothing had happened," she said. "On my break the pit boss complimented me on not making too big a fuss."

Occupational Hazards

Kelly Hass, who left her job as a casino coin-change supervisor to tend bar at the Chelsea Pub, said casino bosses could be friendly with the workers as individuals but ultimately had little regard for their welfare.

"They treat you like a number and ignore you, or treat you like a dog and fire you," Ms. Hass said. "There's absolutely no job protection."

Casino workers, unlike hotel and restaurant workers, have not organized a union and work at the pleasure of management.

"Some dealers have been fired on their break for their attitude—not for something serious like stealing," Mr. Festa said. "Management knows they have people lined up for each job opening."

Despite all that, the hardest part of the job can be boredom. Most casino workers say that blackjack dealers face the most acute problem of keeping focused on repetitive action and the changing faces of players, even with a 20-minute break for every hour worked.

The most serious occupational hazard dealers face is gambling itself. "If you're constantly in the company of high rollers who throw tens of thousands of dollars around, you start thinking your salary is not that great after all," said Harvey R. Fogel, a counselor for compulsive gamblers who has treated scores of casino workers.

"A majority of the dealers won't spend one minute more inside a casino than they have to, but quite a few spend their off-hours at other casinos losing what they had just earned," he said.

"The problem is I can't tell them to quit a $40,000-a-year job to get out of that environment and take a job for less elsewhere," Mr. Fogel added. "And if a dealer goes to his boss and says he's a compulsive gambler, it's worse than admitting you are an alcoholic or a drug addict in their eyes."

A Golden Web

Ms. Perna of Resorts Casino Hotel said that the casinos contract with companies to provide employee assistance programs to help workers with personal problems. Such programs are confidential, she said.

For those who feel trapped in a golden web and do not want to leave the casino industry, there are some alternatives, including taking better jobs as pit bosses or shift supervisors in new casinos that have been opening from Mississippi to Illinois.

Mr. Fogel says he believes the change of scenery may be illusory.

"The ones who are really troubled feel every decision they make is mechanical and every move supervised by someone waiting to pounce on them for screwing up," he said.

And the basic rules of the game, he observed, are the same no matter where one chooses to roll the dice.

SUPERCHARGED BINGO

Andrew Pollack

Andrew Pollack reports in the following selection on a recent innovation in gambling: computerized bingo. Electronic versions of the game enable players to keep track of several bingo cards simultaneously; since participants pay by the card, this innovation enhances potential revenue. According to the author, proponents hope that electronic bingo will increase profits for bingo halls and boost income for charities and nonprofit groups funded by bingo games. Critics maintain, however, that computerized bingo gives its players an unfair advantage over those playing the game the traditional way. Moreover, Pollack points out, lawmakers are unsure about how to regulate computerized bingo. Pollack is a freelance journalist.

Like many women her age, 66-year-old Agnes Myles thinks computers are best left to her grandchildren. "There is the one at home, but I can't be bothered with it," she said.

Except, that is, when playing bingo. At her local bingo hall in Lancaster, Calif., she enters numbers into a small computer that keeps track of dozens of cards for her, more than she could play by hand. The computer can display her best card on its screen and alerts her when she has a winning pattern.

"The more cards you play, the better your chances are," said Mrs. Myles, who started playing bingo decades ago using dried kernels of corn to cover spaces on a cardboard sheet.

Even bingo is going electronic, dragging thousands of grandmothers into the computer age. Employing electronics has been one of the strategies that the nearly 70-year-old pastime, an anchor of fundraising for churches, veterans halls, athletic leagues and other nonprofit groups, is using to try to reinvent itself. And perhaps not a moment too soon.

Casinos and Lotteries Have Hurt Bingo

Bingo and many of the charities that depend on it have been hurt by the spread of other forms of legalized gambling like casinos and state lotteries. Indian tribes, not bound by state regulations that usually limit the prizes a charity can offer to a few hundred dollars, have lured away players by offering bingo with prizes of thousands of dollars a game. The tribes sometimes link several bingo halls together by satellite into one huge game with a jackpot of up to $1 million.

The amount wagered on charitable bingo in the United States fell 2.2 percent in 1996, to $4.04 billion, continuing a decline that began in 1993, according to *International Gaming and Wagering Business* magazine. About 10 percent of what is wagered on bingo ends up going to charity after deducting prizes, expenses and taxes.

In some states, the decline has been far worse. "Thirty-six percent since the bandits moved in across the river," said Gerald Otoupal of the Nebraska Department of Revenue, describing the decline in overall charitable gaming since slot machines, often called one-armed bandits, opened across the Missouri River in Iowa in 1995.

In the state of Washington, Big Brothers and Sisters of Spokane County, which counted on bingo for 95 percent of its budget, saw annual receipts plummet by one-third, or more than $200,000, since 1994, when tribal games opened up outside the city.

There are an estimated 37,000 licensed bingo halls in 46 states—they are illegal in Arkansas, Hawaii, Tennessee and Utah. *The Bingo Bugle*, a newspaper that caters to players, has estimated that there are 1.2 billion visits to bingo halls each year, exceeding even the number of visits to movie theaters.

Over all, after prizes, expenses and taxes are deducted, bingo games raised more than $230 million for charities in 1996 in just the 27 states for which data are available, according to the National Association of Fundraising Ticket Manufacturers, which represents makers of charitable gaming equipment. While that is a drop in the bucket compared with the $150 billion in charitable giving each year, it can be vital to the organizations that depend on it.

Can Electronics Boost Bingo?

Whether electronics can be an elixir for bingo is far from clear. Bingo players are generally not innovative types. Some players sit in the same seat night after night and hate to have their routine interrupted, especially by a machine. Some say it is unfair to those who do not use the computer and changes bingo from a game of some skill into hardcore gambling.

The advantage for the bingo hall is that it allows the players to keep track of far more cards than is humanly possible, increasing potential revenue because players pay by the card. In California, for example, a pack of six cards generally costs $5 to $10. The computers also make it easier for the disabled to play. And there is some hope that computers will impart a more modern image to bingo.

Those who like the computers say that in addition to being able to play more cards, they have more time to socialize or eat. "It's so hard to daub all those cards—you get cross-eyed," said Lili Everard, 67. The computer also prevents a bingo player's worst nightmare: "sleeping a bingo," or having a winning pattern and not realizing it.

But others say that it is boring to have the computer do everything. Indeed, almost all players who use the computers continue to play on paper as well, to keep their hands and minds occupied.

At the bingo hall run by the Big Brothers of Greater Los Angeles in Lancaster, those who do not like the computers or could not afford to buy so many cards complained that the computers gave others an unfair advantage.

"It used to be bingo was a game of ability," said Patricia Pusey, a 45-year-old teacher, who plays only on paper, referring to the skill of keeping track of multiple cards at once. "Now you don't have to track cards. You just have to push buttons."

Since the computers came in, Ms. Pusey said, she has reduced the amount of money she spends, knowing that her chances of winning are lower. Some others have deserted the hall. To limit such complaints, the hall allows the computers to play a maximum of 36 cards, about the upper limit of what a person can play by hand. On a recent Saturday, about one-third of the 206 players were using the computers.

There are also regulatory questions about electronic bingo, which is legal in only about half the states. In 1996, Gov. Roy Romer of Colorado vetoed a bill that would have legalized electronic bingo, in part because it would "make bingo more like other more intensive forms of gambling found in casinos." He also said the state's regulatory system for bingo might not be sophisticated enough to insure that the electronic games were not being manipulated.

Bingo's Transformation

Bingo was made popular by Edwin S. Lowe, a traveling salesman from New York who chanced upon the game being played at a carnival in Atlanta in 1929. At first it was played by covering the numbers on a card with beans and was called beano.

About a decade ago, bingo went through its first technological revolution from hard cards to paper sheets. The squares containing the called numbers are daubed with a round splotch of colored ink using a big marker. A typical player might be able to fill in 6 to 36 cards in the 14 seconds or so before the next number is called.

Compare that with the 600 cards that each player can play at Your Community Bingo in Victorville, Calif., outside Los Angeles, one of the nation's most electronic halls, with 190 networked PC's. The computers, supplied by Gametech International of Tempe, Ariz., fill in the cards automatically as each number is called and display the player's best three cards on the screen. When the player gets the pattern needed to win, the machine plays "You're in the Money" and flashes "Bingo."

Somewhat more typical are the hand-held units like the Power Bingo King, made by Stuart Entertainment of Council Bluffs, Iowa. With these, the player must enter the number called on a keypad one time, and all the cards will be filled in.

How much electronic bingo helps the halls is still unclear. Some halls find they are not worth the extra cost. Ann Perez, the manager of the hall in Lancaster, said revenue had increased by a few hundred dollars a night, a modest sum, since the computers were introduced.

Others report similar results. "By and large it's been a net gain for us," said John Orton, chief financial officer of the American Bingo and Gaming Corporation of Austin, Tex., which operates 18 halls. "It hasn't changed any situation from a failure to a success or a marginal success to a great one."

Regulatory Questions

Pamela A. Perri, executive director of the National Association of Fundraising Ticket Manufacturers, said that bingo could best be helped not by new technology but by relaxing restrictions that hobble its ability to compete with other forms of gaming. There can be restrictions on hours of operation, prizes and prohibitions on hiring of workers.

"I'd like to see a lottery run like a charitable bingo is run," she said. "I'd like to see a lottery sell tickets only six hours a week and offer a top prize of $500."

Charities that run bingo games have organized lobbying groups in several states. And state associations are now banding together to form the Charitable Gaming Federation of America to lobby in Washington.

But while bingo enjoys a more benign image than other forms of gambling, lawmakers still are often reluctant to expand it. Moreover, in part because of its benign image, regulation in many states is lax. The bingo industry is full of illegitimate charities and unscrupulous promoters who organize games for profit and give the charities a pittance.

A Pennsylvania crime commission in 1992 called bingo "a profitable enterprise for organized crime." A South Carolina task force that year found that only one penny of each dollar wagered on bingo in the state was going to charity. In October 1997, the state instituted tougher regulations.

Bingo's best hope for the future might be that the huge baby-boomer generation is nearing the prime bingo-playing years. Computer literate, they might flock to the electronic bingo halls—unless they choose to stay home and play bingo on the Internet, expected by many to be the next wave.

THE DICEY PROSPECT OF CYBER GAMBLING

Leslie Alan Horvitz

Gambling enthusiasts in the United States can now use the Internet to place bets with online casinos and offshore gaming establishments, reports Leslie Alan Horvitz in the following selection. Using money from preestablished accounts, cyber gamblers can access Web sites to bet on bingo, blackjack, craps, video poker, and other games of chance. Some legislators, however, are concerned about the potential for online abuses by dishonest gaming operators as well as the prospect of Internet gambling occurring in states that have outlawed gambling, Horvitz writes. In response to these concerns, many gaming companies are working with lawmakers and regulators to ensure the safety and legality of online gambling. Horvitz is a freelance journalist who frequently contributes to *Insight*, a weekly newsjournal.

As one of America's fastest-growing businesses, gambling seems to have penetrated nearly every corner of the country. State governments routinely look to legalized gambling to bolster revenues—lotteries are ubiquitous. It seemed only a matter of time before gambling moved into cyberspace.

More than 600 sites exist on the World Wide Web in which gamblers can discover the latest spreads on sports contests or learn how to better their winnings at poker. But there's no need to return to the real world to bet on a football team or the ninth race at Belmont. The Web offers sites in which players can try their luck at high-stakes blackjack without ever leaving their computers.

With a couple of clicks of a mouse, on-line gamblers have the opportunity to place bets with casinos operating offshore in countries such as Ireland and Monaco, even if they live in a state such as Utah where gambling is prohibited. Given the growing popularity of a new and anarchic medium like the Internet, laws that long have regulated gambling rapidly are becoming obsolete. While state and federal regulators are alarmed, they are uncertain about what to do about it.

To get an idea of what the Web offers gambling enthusiasts—the industry prefers the word *gaming*—one only has to call up the *Rolling Good Times* home page. *RGT*, as it's known, . . . boasts 25,000 readers who regularly access the 130,000 pages of material available on its site. For six months, *RGT* offered a blackjack school, advising card players that "virtually all blackjack games can be beaten—and quite a few are really a waste of your time since the possible rewards are outweighed by the risks involved in playing them." *RGT* also offers features on craps, video poker, sports betting, handicapping ("the ponies"), greyhound racing ("the puppies") and on-line gambling. There even is a site called the "Show Me Pages" devoted to "a collection of Missouri gambling activities."

Gamblers who want to bet can access sites such as Sports International, based in Antigua, West Indies, putting down money from a preestablished account. There also is a national Internet bingo game (operated by 50 American Indian tribes twice a day Monday through Saturday) that relies on a "proxy-play service": An individual ("proxy") in a bingo hall purportedly plays the card on behalf of the player. A nationwide lottery on the Internet is due in 1997.

The most sophisticated gambling on the Internet takes the form of on-line casinos (usually located offshore) that use complex mathematical formulas and algorithms to determine the outcome of every "virtual" roll of the dice or spin of the wheel. Internet Gaming Technologies Inc., for example, is promoting a "telephony-based 'virtual casino' entertainment which offers a full line of Las Vegas–style casino games, on-line shopping, chat lounges, member parties and travel incentives." So far, few of these Internet casinos and sports-book operations are up and running, mainly because of technical hitches. A player who takes a hit during a game of blackjack, for example, often has to wait 10 to 20 seconds while the home computer communicates with the host computer. But no one expresses any doubt that these obstacles can be overcome.

Digital Cash

In contrast to traditional casinos, where bettors gamble with chips for which they've paid in cash, on-line casinos still are struggling with various forms of payment. (This is a problem that affects many aspects of the Internet where goods are offered for sale.) Many users are reluctant to provide financial information over the Internet for fear of theft or fraud. To meet this challenge, several companies are developing a variety of on-line payment systems, all of which rely on the concept of "digital cash." Digital cash, unlike the real thing, usually takes the form of credit or debit cards which cannot be accessed unless the holder enters the correct access code. These cards also can be encoded to contain relevant information, like the age of the holder, to prevent underage gambling.

Security isn't the only problem for the virtual gaming industry.

Players have no way to verify a casino operator's identity, much less to determine if he or she is honest or ethical. According to government sources, individuals who could not otherwise receive licenses from legal gaming jurisdictions are involved in the operation of Internet gambling sites. In the absence of regulation, there also is no guarantee that an operator won't tinker with the algorithms to make the outcomes more favorable to the house. Nor is there anything to prevent an operator from simply taking the money and running.

Regulating On-Line Gambling

In June 1995, the National Association of Attorneys General, or NAAG, authorized the creation of the Internet Working Group, charged with "developing a response to various issues involving Internet activities." Until now, gambling has been regulated on a state-by-state basis, with little uniformity and minimal federal oversight. But state laws that extend jurisdiction over an offshore casino operator, for instance, are clumsy and ineffectual. In some states, it is illegal to advertise a gambling operation, but it is questionable whether courts will find jurisdiction over advertisers who take no subscription applications or payments.

Some regulators see phone-fraud laws as a precedent for on-line gambling regulation. They also suggest that cases could be built on the basis of existing consumer-protection laws. . . . Extradition, too, is held out as a legal recourse, but many countries do not have reciprocal extradition treaties with the United States.

Hoping to call attention to potential abuses, the NAAG issued a report that recommended new state laws and tougher federal regulations to cover gambling on the Internet. Since the report was released, however, little progress has been made to this effect. Alan R. Kesner, Minnesota's attorney general who chairs the NAAG subcommittee on Internet gambling, admits little work will be done until after the 1996 elections. And even if new or amended laws are on the books, he points out, that doesn't necessarily mean a solution is in sight. Laws against gambling run into the same problems laws against drugs do. "The difficulty is enforceability."

The Future of Cyber Gambling

Not surprisingly, many of those associated with the gaming industry aren't convinced there is a problem, at least not on the scale envisioned by NAAG. "The report lacks credibility from almost the opening line," contends Glenn Barry, a lottery management consultant who writes a regular column for *RGT*. He claims states are afraid that they won't get their share of taxes from gambling taking place beyond their jurisdiction.

"The writers of this report are trying to create a 'now' threat when it is still a 'maybe,'" says Barry, pointing out that a player has to go to great lengths to gamble on-line: First of all, he or she needs a computer. The player has to find a service provider, then he or she has to learn Netscape (a popular Web browser), then the player has to "wade through pages and pages of 'Net noise' to find a site to gamble." He says he doubts whether more than a small percentage of the population ever will use the Net for gambling, intimating that it might come down to a few gambling-deprived souls in Utah and other states in which gambling is illegal.

This is not to suggest that government regulators and the gaming industry necessarily conflict when it comes to the future of gambling on the Internet. Kesner says the NAAG is working closely with representatives of the industry to prevent abuses on-line. And evidence indicates that as companies seek to expand their gaming enterprises to the Internet, they increasingly are anxious to allay legal concerns. When a consortium announced plans recently to set up an on-line casino called Emerald Riviera (based in Ireland, naturally), it was quick to add that it also was establishing a code of ethics "which mandates such items as background checks, the requirement of local licensing and the commitment not to market where Internet wagering is illegal." It promised that all algorithms used to produce game outcomes would be audited by a Big Six accounting firm.

"We've been working hard to educate legislators about this new form of home entertainment and how to build in safeguards," says Kendall Lang of Casino World Holdings, a company investing in Emerald Riviera. "It's our intent to show regulators how this can be done legally." Says Kesner, "The legitimate gaming industry recognizes that bad blood and bad actors have a taint that they need to avoid."

CHAPTER 2

PERSPECTIVES ON GAMBLING

WHY I GAMBLE:
PLEASURE AND ITS PERILS

Daniel Seligman

In the following selection, Daniel Seligman defines gambling as a pleasurable activity that can generate profits when games are played repetitively. As an example, he describes how he gambles at horseracing: He places small, weekly bets on several different combinations of possible first-, second-, and third-place finishers; over the course of several months or years he may win big only a few times, but these large payoffs are more than enough to cover his gambling expenses. If consistently played, fair games will result in frequent small losses and occasional large—and profitable—wins, Seligman writes. Seligman is a columnist for *Fortune* and the author of *A Question of Intelligence*.

This article is driving me crazy. First, it is sinking in, after several days of staring at the title above, that the issues it raises are more complex than posited when I accepted the assignment. Second, the passage of those several days has created a certain tension between two cherished goals: 1) assured manuscript delivery by vouchsafed deadline date and 2) unstinting participation in this month's [March 1995] poker game, only two days off as I write.

Furthermore, I start out knowing that no matter what story line I come up with, a significant fraction of readers will unbudgingly go on thinking that gambling is bad. Several years ago, I was called by an investment-banker friend who asked if I would mind having lunch with her and a client—a conservative intellectual who happened to run a steel company, was said to admire my *Fortune* column, and shared my hard-line perspective on numerous issues of the day. Feeling flattered, I accepted and, until the very end of our meeting, felt I had come to know a kindred spirit. But as we were leaving La Côte Basque, my newfound friend asked a bit diffidently about the numerous references in the column to casinos and race tracks. Was it really true, he asked, that I hung around such places? I said it was, and he said, "Oh," looking embarrassed. Social conservatives tend to see gambling as a big negative on the values scorecard. Intellectuals feel it betokens a want of seriousness. Economists of every persuasion go around arguing that it is "unproductive"—that, in the words of Paul Samuelson, "it involves simple *sterile transfers of money or goods* between individuals creating no new money or goods." The italics are Paul's, as is the familiar refusal to accept that gambling is terrific entertainment.

Gambling has been a major theme in my life since approximately age twenty, and I seem to have come by the habit honestly. My father was a heavy sports bettor for much of his life, and my mother was eternally loving and attentive—precisely the kind of mother who, according to Sigmund Freud, leaves men feeling forever lucky as they march through life. Anybody wishing to observe several score characters radiating this state of grace in unison has only to board the 8 P.M. flight from Los Angeles to Las Vegas. The atmosphere features loud hoots and unconstrained hilarity. The 1:45 A.M. flight back is much more subdued; to be sure, the guys have had a long day.

Betting as a Form of Saving

There are several things to be said for gambling, the first of which is: You really might win. Furthermore, you might win big. In fact, you almost certainly will win big if you hang in there and structure your bets properly. Here I am sidling up to one of my two theoretical contributions to the economics of gambling: the counterintuitive view of long-shot betting as a form of saving.

The saving process, as we all know, involves the conversion of a stream of income into a lump of capital. A man who takes $100 out of his weekly paycheck and puts it under his mattress might get criticized for failing to maximize investment returns, but no economist would deny that the $5,200 he had accumulated after a year was the result of saving.

Now imagine another chap—one who also wishes to convert $100 a week into $5,200 but feels he is entitled to a few kicks along the way. Since he luckily lives in downtown Las Vegas, it is convenient for him to visit Binion's Horseshoe casino once a week. His plan on these visits is to throw $100 on the table each time, hoping eventually to get lucky and win something like $5,200. Unfortunately, no casinos offer 51 to 1 bets to low rollers, but there are a number of casino games in which you get huge long-shot payoffs by winning five or six times in a row and letting your profits ride. If you know what you are doing and elect to play blackjack with a single deck (possible at Binion's but hard to find on the Strip), you are essentially in a fair game, i.e., the house edge is minimal (and the casino depends for its profits on the inept). So if you sit down at the $100 table and win six hands in a row, you will leave the table with something like $6,400. The chance of winning an even-money bet six times in a row is only 1.56 per cent, but the chance of winning *one such bet* in 52 weekly visits is 56 per cent.

So you are favored to win at least once a year, and if you do so, your lump will be substantially larger than that of our mattress man.

It is possible to imagine various real-world problems arising out of this approach to nest-egg building, but the basic conception is rock solid. If you repetitively play a fair game, and structure your bets so as to generate frequent losses and occasional big wins, then you are converting income into capital. Indeed you are doing that even if the game is not quite fair. If your weekly savings budget was getting tossed on the craps table instead of the blackjack table, you would possibly be fighting a house edge of 0.6 per cent, but you would still be favored (53 per cent this time) to convert $100 into $6,400 at least once a year.

Gambling at the Racetrack

My own preferred and most successful form of saving has featured ninth-race triples, also known as trifectas, at New York's Aqueduct and Belmont racetracks. A triple is a long-shot bet, requiring one to pick the first three horses to cross the finish line, in order. If you buy a triple "box," which consists of six bets featuring all combinations of your three horses, you don't have to worry about the order. A triple box costs $12, and my standard bet is four or five boxes, all on horses selected randomly by a BASIC program lovingly conceived for this purpose alone. (It prompts you for the number of horses in the race, the program numbers of any scratches, and the number of boxes you wish to buy, then spits out your selections.) If 12 steeds are running, a bettor with five boxes going has a 2.3 per cent chance of hitting a triple, and if he plays this game once a week, he has a 70 per cent chance of hitting at least once a year, and over the years he has a serious expectation of latching onto some sizable payoffs. Since 1986, when I first began putting the results of my gambling into a spreadsheet, I have had around 300 betting days that featured triples, of which only a handful were winners. But these included payoffs of $14,611, $11,225, $9,644, $3,794, and $3,394. And even though New York racetracks have a horrifying edge of 25 per cent on triple bets— i.e., payments to winners represent only about 75 per cent of the money bet—the spreadsheet shows me way ahead of the game. So it is fairly easy to view the recurrent losses of $48 or $60 as deposits into a savings account.

A Positive Economic Effect

Possibly you are wondering about my other contribution to economic theory. It was built on an insight gleaned from our monthly poker game. This began in 1953 as a low-stakes limit game but soon upgraded itself to table stakes (in which a player can bet any amount up to the total of chits and chips he had in front of him when the deal started). The greybeards still in the game know there is a possibility of winning or losing as much as $1,000 in an evening, but a more likely outcome is a swing under $500. An interesting thing about those figures is that they were far larger back in the Fifties, when we were all much poorer. It was then common to win or lose over $2,500 in one session—around $14,000 in today's prices. Whatever else it was doing, the game in those years clearly served as the great monthly adventure in our lives, one that was doubly wonderful in that, unlike Antarctic exploration or rappelling in the Rockies, it came with no physical risks or material discomfort. In those days, we tended to play all night, drink quite a lot while doing so, then go out for breakfast before wandering off to a barber and the office. Once, in 1958, I personally managed to lose $1,600—at a time when my annual salary was $16,000, I had no savings to speak of, and I was the sole support of a family of four. Breakfasting with the gang at a Lexington Avenue coffee shop, I did my best to feign insouciance over the night's results, but the refrain that kept rattling in my head was: How in hell do I get out of this mess?

The answer, revealed to me in the ensuing months, is at the heart of my theoretical contribution, which states: Gambling has a positive effect on economic activity. A significant fraction of the winners will regard their loot as "found money" and rush to spend it, and quite a few of the losers will feel an instant, urgent need to augment earnings, which in my case meant toiling mightily in the freelance [writing] market. Please do not draw any inferences from the fact that I am still so toiling.

About the problem mentioned in the first paragraph: The guys instantly agreed to postpone the March game. To be sure, they are getting old.

I Won the Powerball Lottery

Pam Hiatt, as told to Shana Aborn

Idaho state lottery winner Pam Hiatt discusses the effects of her multimillion-dollar winnings in the following selection. A young divorced woman pregnant with her first child, Hiatt lived with her parents and worked several part-time jobs to make ends meet before winning the lottery. With her new riches, she was able to buy a ranch, purchase cars for her family, and secure college funds for her son and nephews. Her fortune was not trouble-free, however—Hiatt explains that she initially had problems managing her income and that she has become wary about meeting new people who may be after her money. All in all, though, Hiatt is happy with her new financial security. Shana Aborn is an associate editor of *Ladies' Home Journal*.

"Honey, come here." Jarene, the convenience-store clerk, was beckoning to me with a huge smile on her face. Even though I had just made a quick stop to check my lottery ticket, I couldn't imagine what she was so excited about. Well, maybe I got a small prize, I thought. Maybe a thousand dollars. I joined Jarene behind the counter, and she shouted, "You won!"

That's how I found out in June 1995 that I was a multimillionaire—$87.5 million richer, to be exact—at the age of twenty-six.

My heart started pounding, and all I could say was, "Oh my gosh, oh my gosh! No way!" Because I was eight months pregnant, Jarene tried to make me sit down, but I kept pacing back and forth. I finally calmed down enough to call my mom and tell her to meet me. She didn't believe my story at first, but by the time she got to the store, she was trembling. We hugged each other as she cried, "I can't believe you won!"

Hard to Believe

My stepdad, Randy, my sister, Juanita, and brother, Andy, were there to congratulate me when Mom and I drove home. My other siblings—my older brother, Greg, and my other brother, Kelly—thought I was joking, and I had to convince them I was serious before they agreed to come over to our house. Once we were together, I told everyone, "The first thing I want to do is buy each of you a new car."

No way was I sleeping that night. My mind was going a hundred miles an hour. Of course, I was incredibly happy, but I was also afraid that I was being given this good luck only to have something terrible come of it. What if I lost my family and friends because they were fighting over the money? Then the prize would mean nothing to me.

And it was hard to believe that all the financial problems I'd worried about for so long were over. My family has always had to work hard, and we never had many luxuries. To earn college benefits, I served in the Army and then in the Idaho National Guard, but money was still tight when I enrolled at Boise State University in 1993 to study political science. To pay the bills, I juggled part-time jobs.

As if things weren't complicated enough, I became pregnant in the fall of 1994. Ending the pregnancy wasn't an option—I very much wanted to be a mother. (I'm divorced, but I have no children from that marriage.) Marrying Todd, my boyfriend, wasn't an option, either, because our relationship was starting to fall apart. I was frustrated and exhausted from my busy schedule.

In May of 1995, I had reluctantly left my apartment and moved back home with my mom and stepdad. I hated having to live off my parents at my age, but my priority was to finish school, and I wouldn't be able to do that and keep working once the baby was born. More than anything, I was upset because I couldn't give my child everything he or she deserved. The only space we had for a nursery was a drab, unfinished basement room that even a new coat of paint couldn't improve.

Dreams of Winning

I firmly believe in the power of prayer, so every night I would ask God for a way out of my financial dilemma. "I'm not asking to win the lottery," I'd say. (I really did put it that way.) "I don't want millions of dollars. I just need an opportunity so I can afford a little studio apartment."

Still, even if I didn't pray for it, I did sometimes dream about winning the lottery. Idaho is one of twenty states along with Washington, D.C., that sponsors the Powerball lotto, and the jackpot often reaches tens of millions. I would buy a ticket about once a week, always playing the current ages of my family: 7 and 20 for Andy and Kelly, 21 for Juanita, 26 for me, 27 for Greg and 45 for Mom. (She was forty-six that year, but the Powerball numbers don't go that high.)

I played those numbers on Saturday, June 4, 1995, when I stopped at the Jacksons Food Store to pick up some breakfast on my way to my annual training with the National Guard. Andy had just celebrated his eighth birthday on Friday, but luckily for me, I already had my lotto card prepared and didn't feel like going to the trouble of filling out a new one.

Once I won, there was so much to take care of in such a short time. In a funny twist of fate, I hired the attorney who used to be my boss to handle my legal affairs.

Then I went to the Idaho State Lottery office, where I filled out forms and underwent a background check as part of the verification process. Pat Reilly, the communications director, told me I could pick up my first of twenty annuity payments of $4.37 million that Monday, and we arranged a press conference for the same time.

Once the press conference was over, I kept my promise to buy cars for my family. I didn't care if the check cleared my bank account on time; I wanted to do it now! I got myself a black BMW 325i, but I later traded it in for a Toyota LandCruiser. A week or so after that, my mom told me to go out and do something fun for myself. So I bought a Porsche.

Next, I went house hunting so I could move in before the baby came. The realtors showed me some huge mansions in the area, but my life was overwhelming enough as it was. I needed a house that I could call home right away. I chose a $180,000 three-bedroom ranch in a good neighborhood, and the first thing I bought for it was a nice set of nursery furniture.

A Lot of Headaches

Everyone was fascinated by the young millionaire mom, and I got lots of interview requests—including appearances on *The Late Show with David Letterman* and *Good Morning America*, two of my favorite shows.

That was the fun part of being a lottery winner, but there were a lot of headaches, too. I learned more about finance during that first week than I *ever* wanted to know. You have to think about taxes, taxes, taxes. After I bought all those cars, my attorneys freaked out and quickly taught me that I'd have to pay gift taxes on large sums of money or expensive gifts. More than $1 million of my winnings each year goes to income tax. Then there's estate planning, retirement planning, liability insurance, life insurance, investments and college funds for my baby, Andy and my nephews.

The excitement had just begun to die down when I suddenly had something else to focus on. On the morning of June 21, 1995, three weeks before my due date, I thought my water was breaking. I went to the hospital, where I was examined and sent home. Three hours later, I got a terrible backache that turned out to be labor pain. My mom and stepdad barely got me back to the hospital in time for the arrival of Nicholas Jacob. I discovered what true love really was when I first held my son.

Now Nicholas is an adorable ten-month-old who's the most important person in my life. He has my blond hair and blue eyes, a sweet disposition and more clothes than I do!

While Nicholas will grow up knowing that we live comfortably, I don't want him to know exactly how rich we are until he's a young adult. By then, I hope the values I've instilled will be so solid that wealth won't even be an issue for him. A modest regular allowance will help him learn money management.

It's a lesson I'm still learning myself. The desk in my home office is overflowing with paperwork. Of the money left after taxes and savings, several hundred dollars a month goes toward bills and attorneys' fees. For my personal needs, my financial advisers have given me a monthly budget of $10,000. At first I thought that was too generous, but it's amazing how much you can spend when you have the cash. I don't buy nearly as much now as I did in the beginning, though. I splurge mostly on clothes for Nicholas, meals out with friends and a few extras, like a diamond ring and family trips.

Having Fun and Doing Good for Others

Sometimes I feel guilty about buying so many frivolous things. But then again, as my mom says, this isn't supposed to be a serious, stressful time for me; I should be having fun. I'm not spending everything on myself, either; my winnings will also be used to do good for others. I've already established a nonworking foundation, which means that, although the foundation itself does not actively work for a cause, it is used to donate funds to organizations that do, such as the Red Cross. Once I'm out of school, I'd like to start a business of some kind to help support the foundation.

Maybe later I'll even go after a more creative dream, like becoming an actor or stand-up comedian. I could be the only comic who pays the audience to laugh!

The downside to being suddenly rich is that you have to be careful about people's motives. When I first won, my mail was filled with not only congratulatory notes but also investment offers and hard-luck letters. I'm wary about meeting new people, because I'm afraid they might just be interested in the money. I'm lucky that my true friends have honestly been wonderful about not treating me differently.

An Ordinary Life

Most people wouldn't believe how ordinary my life is. I'm out of the National Guard and in school full-time, so my typical day consists of going to classes, doing chores and playing with Nicholas. (A sitter watches him when I'm at school. My idea of a great time on a Friday night isn't club hopping but hanging out at home with my best friend, Sheila, eating take-out Chinese food and watching *The X-Files*.)

I'm not dating anyone special, though I've had some marriage offers in the mail and friends are always trying to fix me up. I'd like to get married again, but I think my next husband would have to be someone strong enough not to be intimidated by my wealth. . . .

For now, I'm taking everything slowly. The money will still be there tomorrow and the next year and the next. Whatever happens in the end, what's important to me is being known for who I am and what I've done in life, not for having a bank account with lots of zeros.

The one thing I'll never buy with my millions is another lottery ticket. I've been so blessed that I'll never ask for anything again.

WHEN I WON MILLIONS, I LOST MYSELF

Tracy Adinolfi

Riches do not buy happiness, claims Tracy Adinolfi as she examines how her Pennsylvania lottery winnings have changed her life. Although Adinolfi enjoys being able to spend money, she is disturbed by her isolation from friends and family with whom she no longer shares much in common. She fears that her friends are jealous and resentful of her luck; moreover, Adinolfi often feels that she lacks ambition and enthusiasm because she no longer needs to work for a living. Only impending motherhood—not money—has given Adinolfi a sense of purpose in her life.

"Tracy! You've got it! You hit it!" My fiancé, John, ran into the kitchen, grabbed me around the waist and picked me up, screaming that I'd won the lottery. John loves to tease me, so of course I didn't believe him—until I matched the numbers for myself. It was true! Seven random numbers, picked on just the right day—July 22, 1992—in just the right state—Pennsylvania, where we were visiting relatives—had landed me $8.9 million.

Could a 21-year-old girl from Brooklyn who was working a minimum-wage job with TWA one day be rich the next? I was shocked. Add to it the jolt of being newly engaged (John had proposed only the day before), and you can imagine how dazed I was. I felt like the luckiest girl in the world.

The day after I won, I didn't go in to work—no phone call, no apology. I just didn't show up. Sure, it was irresponsible of me, but I didn't care. Shopping became my new nine-to-five job. I relished the shocked expressions of stuck-up saleswomen when I slapped my gold card on the counter. You see, I grew up the youngest of eight children in a two-bedroom apartment. If we got holes in our shoes, we'd put cardboard in the bottoms until the next payday. So I loved seeing how the other half lived.

As for my wedding, I'd always wanted a huge *Father of the Bride*–type reception, but never imagined that I'd be able to afford one. The day I got married, I just stared at the roses, the ice sculptures, my ten bridesmaids in their gorgeous chiffon dresses, and felt like a princess.

Disturbing Changes

But the fairy tale ended fast. It was disturbing how things changed between me and my siblings, who seemed to consider my house an ATM. We all live within four blocks of one another, so there was no escaping running into my family. I became everyone's backup financial security when paychecks couldn't cover the bills. Recently, I had to put a stop to that. It was getting to the point where I was paying rents on a semi-regular basis. We argued about it at first, but now they're beginning to see it my way.

Meanwhile, I no longer seem to have much in common with people I've grown up with. Just the other night, we went to a bar that used to be our hangout, and they were griping about their bosses. I had absolutely nothing to say. I couldn't exactly talk about the manicures I get while they're slaving at the office or the swimming pool we're having built in the backyard. I don't want to feed the resentment and jealousy that's already there, making me feel like I should apologize for having money. When the bar bill comes, no one reaches for it. They just look at me.

No Sure Ticket to Happiness

It's amazing to realize how many assumptions people make when you've got money. Deep down, they believe that money makes you happy. My father died of cancer a year after I won, and I'll never forget how people reacted. At first, they were sympathetic, but after a few months went by and I was still depressed, they'd say things like, "You have everything, so why are you still so unhappy?" If money could bring my father back, then, yeah, I'd be happy. Just because you have money doesn't mean all of life gets easier.

Or that you feel any more secure. Now and then, I even wonder if John really loves me the way I am, or if he's more dependent on my bank account than on me. Thank goodness he proposed the night *before* I won; people can talk all they want, but *I* know he didn't marry me for my money.

True, for a year and a half after I won, John didn't work, either. All we did was hang around the house all day and take cruises. John got so bored, he decided to become a fireman—he'd always wanted to be one but had ended up working odd construction jobs instead. He's a lot happier now. I seriously wonder whether I would be happier if I worked, too. Whenever I go into Manhattan and see women my age rushing to work, I feel as if the world is passing me by. Then I get angry with myself and hate the fact that I have no ambition and no drive because I make $342,000 a year doing absolutely nothing. Still, I can't shake the idea that work is something one *has* to do—not something that one wants to do.

What I really want to do is be a mom. And I'll get my wish in a few months, because John and I are having a baby. Now that I'm pregnant, I finally have a purpose, something to talk about, to plan for. Thinking about being a parent has given me a bit more of a sense of who I am, although I worry that my child will end up being my *life*.

It's been several years since I won. I have a new, fully decorated house, more shoes than Imelda Marcos and snapshots of John and me in Hawaii. But my most prized possession—my future baby—is the one thing that money could never buy.

EVERYONE WINS AND LOSES ALONE

George Packer

In the following piece, George Packer examines the significance of the popularity of gambling. Reflecting on his experiences at Foxwoods Casino in Connecticut, Packer maintains that gambling is a compulsive, self-absorbed activity that alienates people from each other. Furthermore, he points out, many states have become "dealers"; that is, they rely on revenue from betting as an essential supplement to taxes. This state dependence on gambling revenues has intensified Americans' sense of estrangement from their government, he concludes. Packer is the author of *The Village of Waiting*, a memoir, and *The Half Man*, a novel.

Economists have begun using the term "winner-take-all economics" to describe the fact that the salaries of investment bankers, software designers, and basketball players continue to rise while the wages of photocopy attendants and paramedics stagnate or fall toward the official poverty level. The phrase suggests that in the present economy millions of people are bound to "lose," and evokes the image of a society badly divided between the successful and the luckless, whose fates have little or nothing to do with one another.

A Casino of the Middle Class

A good place to gauge this state of affairs is Foxwoods, the turquoise and purple casino palace that rises like Oz from a small patch of Indian land in the prosaic hills of southeastern Connecticut. The world's largest, Foxwoods is the great casino of the American middle class. It has none of Vegas's slick glamour or high-rolling dangers; it isn't bleak and malodorous like Atlantic City; it lacks the vacationland lure of the new Mississippi riverboats. Its vast parking lot is jammed with the vehicles of local cafeteria workers, contractors, retirees. Inside, the enormous gaming rooms swarm every night of the year. There are disproportionate numbers of smokers and also, since gambling is a leisure activity that doesn't require legs, people in wheelchairs. Under the purple ceiling half-globes that hide surveillance cameras, winners look nearly as grim-faced as losers. Cocktail waitresses glide by, wearing feathers in their hair and skimpy buckskin costumes that ride

Reprinted from George Packer, "Read 'em and Weep," *Dissent*, Summer 1995, by permission of *Dissent* magazine.

high up their hips, but the men seem not to notice. The intensity of gambling leaves no room for an aphrodisiac.

Around the tables a laconic code prevails. It's hard to pick out couples or families or groups of friends, as if, once through the glass doors and past the men in security jackets, those ties dissolve and everyone becomes a separate individual.

Everyone wins and loses alone. The noise never varies and never stops—the clatter of roulette wheels and click of dice and the mechanical spin and clank of slot machines. Gradually you discern human voices too, but they have a scattered, random sound, with no collective focus, directed not at other people but at cards and dice and other inanimate objects.

The Slots Room

In the giant slots room, just beyond the sign with an 800 number for Gamblers Anonymous, a thousand machines all seem to be spinning at the same time. The first time I walked into its vast low expanse, with the ceaseless mechanical din, the people standing shoulder to shoulder at rows of machines into which they were feeding quarters by the bucketful, the room gave me a sense of déjà vu. It was like a fantastically lit-up, garish makeover of an old factory floor.

The previous year, a hundred miles north in Lowell, Massachusetts, I'd visited an abandoned yarn mill. It stood locked in ice, its shattered windows having looked out on the Merrimack River since the beginning of industrial capitalism in the 1820s. When I toured it the mill had been empty for a decade, and the last owner seemed to have fled before an invading army. In the offices, boxes of time cards and filled-in production tables; in the tubs of dye, junked machinery; on the shop floors, busted crates and stacks of great empty spools. Rows of spinning machines still crowded together on the pine flooring, mechanical rods connecting them to the crank shafts overhead. My guide through these five stories of cold and silent gloom was Donald Marchand, the caretaker, an aging bachelor in a corduroy baseball cap and flannel shirt buttoned over his large belly up to his throat. His father and brothers had worked in the mill; he himself had lived his whole life within a few blocks of it. "Lots of people went up these stairs," Donald Marchand muttered as we climbed. "Thousands and thousands."

The slots room at Foxwoods seems a long way from that ghost of deindustrialization. Play, not work, is going on here, and the jobs that exist—croupier, money-changer, waitress—belong to the post-industrial nonunion service economy that has taken the place of manufacturing. But the longer you stay, the more this vision of leisure and freedom comes to resemble compulsion and work. The grandmothers, the old men in hats, the young men and women in sweat-suits pull levers and push buttons as fast and repetitively and with as little expression as textile workers at their looms. When a payoff clatters out, the quarters get scooped up and go right back into the slots. I myself have trouble walking past these machines, with their lurid colors and false promises, without groping in my pocket for coins.

The Losers

I prefer the poker table to the games of chance. Downstairs, amid the stale smoke, you compete against other fallible human beings instead of long odds. The dealer in his faux-Indian embroidered shirt sweeps away the ante; eight hopefuls scramble for the rest. With each new hand of seven-card stud there is the familiar rhythm of a thrill rising, the thrill that accounts for my being here, the seductive pleasure of self-interested risk and eternally springing hope (for nothing, not even utopia, can take the place of how the nerves jump when I stake money and pride against you and chance, or how the blood warms when I trick you into folding your better hand, or how the vision dims when your last hole card turns out to have completed a flush). With the fourth or fifth card of most hands the thrill ebbs away; but sometimes it begins building to a climax of mute pain or ecstasy.

The last time I played, I lost more money than I'd meant to wager, on two heartbreaking hands. Before I had time to study the faces of my opponents I was cleaned out. My last dollar went for the dealer's tip: as I rose he wished me good night. I walked back upstairs in a daze, past the teepee display and the sound-and-light show of the giant Indian archer, and found myself among the blackjack and roulette tables, where dealers and croupiers kept sweeping piles of chips away from stunned-faced players.

And suddenly I had the only thought that could have consoled me at that moment: All these people are losers. I'm not the only one—they're all losing too. Look at that emaciated woman who just stepped up to the roulette wheel: two minutes, twenty dollars, now she's wandering away, better luck elsewhere. Maybe a few were winning: at every table one or two players warily clutched stacks of chips like dogs with stolen hunks of meat. But the vast majority were losing. If everyone had to exit through a door under the neon sign "Winners" or "Losers," the line at the latter would be five times longer. Then at least they would stop being random individuals down on the night, and could become a community of losers, and look into one another's eyes with a shock of recognition: You too?

The cashier in the food court told me she'd been working at Foxwoods for over a year—a long time, she added, compared to most. I asked if it was a stressful job.

"Well, there's a lot of people. A lot of *angry* people."

The Citizen as Player

In 1993 Americans spent 330 billion dollars on legal gambling—more than on books, movies, amusement arcades, and recorded music put together. Which is to say, Americans are now losing in enormous numbers.

In some parts of the country, gambling is the only growth industry. One cold morning in Detroit a rumor of a casino that would probably never be approved drew ten thousand job applicants. But the explosion in state lotteries, bingo halls, and casinos is mainly due to the inability of governments across the country to raise enough money the traditional way, through taxes, to keep the schools open and pick up the trash. And at first glance gambling seems like a fair way to bring it in. Instead of a compulsory tax on everyone's income, the government runs its lotteries and gets a share of the casino's take. It's voluntary; it's a kind of free market; it even dispenses rough justice in rewarding the blackjack player's skill and punishing the craps addict. Only the willing contribute—no citizen is obliged by law to stand at a video poker machine and pump it full of quarters.

The replacement of taxes by take suggests a new twist in the citizen's relation to the state, one strongly aligned with the tendency of contemporary life toward fragmentation, the rule of markets, risk over security. Instead of taxpayers, citizens become players, white-knuckled with self-interest, each trying his or her luck against the others and the house. The winners go on vacation, the losers pay for Medicaid and bridge repairs. Instead of the tax collector, in the old aphorism a leveler second only to death, we have the state as dealer, wearing an implacable mask of indifference to the citizen-players who happen to sit at its table, giving and taking according to the most irrational measure available, blind, mindless, responsible for nothing, just the invisible hand rolling, spinning, dealing.

Enshrining Self-Interest

The state as dealer enshrines self-interest at the level of an official national trait, the way the uniformed extorter represents the state in Haiti and the mild-faced bureaucrat in Sweden. Public revenue becomes the take on millions of separate self-interests colliding in an enormous room, the result determined by modest skill and large amounts of luck—not a bad representation of individual fates, but as a principle of collective destiny it bears some resemblance to the town in Shirley Jackson's story "The Lottery," where every year a citizen whose name has been drawn is stoned to death.

Does it matter how the government collects its money? Taxes, which are so unpopular that politicians would rather gamble with high-risk securities than raise them, are one measure of a citizen's stake in the common life of a democracy. Jury duty almost never happens; military service isn't compulsory; voting is an option more and more people pass up. The requirement that citizens surrender some fraction of their income every year should remind us that private happiness partly depends on public institutions and a web of relations to one another whose center is the government. Taxes measure our willingness to acknowledge that in a sense we're all in it together.

But maybe it isn't true; maybe in the new economy the winners can devote enough of their winnings to insulating themselves from the depredations of the losers that their lives will actually be better off in isolation. The chaos of public schools, the corruption of public officials, the filth of public bathrooms: the word itself suggests poverty and danger and failure. To win is to privatize. A sense of connection is what successful people avoid.

I know the private pleasure of gambling, but I also know that the state as dealer won't solve the problem of Americans' notorious alienation from government; it simply avoids the problem. In the end, take instead of taxes will deepen the alienation, making government more remote from the mass of Americans, more corrupt, less accountable, less just.

THE SADNESS OF A CITY

William C. Graham

William C. Graham briefly describes his visit to Atlantic City, where he finds himself distressed by the garishness of its casinos and the bleak spectacle of middle-class and poor people repetitively playing slot machines. He concludes that the fortunes spent on gambling and on building casinos would be better spent on helping the poor. Graham is a Catholic priest and an associate professor of religious studies at Caldwell College in Caldwell, New Jersey.

Though I've lived several years in New York, I had until recently successfully avoided any excursion to Atlantic City. When a recent visitor arrived from the Midwest, however, we planned a two-day trip to that ocean-front hot spot on the Jersey Shore. We stayed but two hours and headed quickly back to New York City and Harlem, where the plastic is not so offensive nor the sleaze so repugnant, where even rip-offs seem a bit more respectful, and the poor, while marginalized, are not mocked.

An amazing number of tour buses (10,197,884 in 1996) filled with eager gamblers speed down the Garden State Parkway, where the law sets 55 miles per hour as the maximum. I saw troopers stop any number of cars along the way, but didn't see any buses pulled over, even though I tailed a couple at speeds close to 15 m.p.h. above the limit. They are astonishing in number, those speeding buses, and carry cargo important to the economy of the casinos.

Donald Trump's Taj Mahal has a bus depot on the ground floor, just one of many spots in town where buses land, that is bigger and busier than most any bus station in a city many times the size of the relatively small Atlantic City, population 37,000. I checked on an expected bus from Caldwell in northeastern New Jersey. Three coaches had arrived from that tiny hamlet within minutes of each other. These folks are among the 37 million annual visitors to Atlantic City who, in 1996, dropped $39,963,075,000 in casino hotel activity. This multitude of visitors makes Atlantic City the most popular tourist destination in the United States.

Much is written about the sadness of Atlantic City itself, a depress-

Reprinted from William C. Graham, "The Sadness of a City," *America*, July 5, 1997, by permission of the author.

ing, poverty-stricken place where the ocean front is given to T-shirt shops and casinos dot the boardwalk. I have lived for four years in Harlem and am more accustomed to the face of poverty than I want to be, but I found Atlantic City's poverty distressing from another perspective. The ocean and the souvenirs are not the real draw there. The casinos are. And what a disturbing reality they are. The Taj Mahal is so far removed from any real sense of grandeur or majesty that any right thinking developer should have been embarrassed to propose it. But I can't ask who might find such a place attractive; there seem to be millions of them. In 1996 Atlantic City's hotel occupancy rate was 89.5 percent, with 3,368,871 room-nights filled.

The Taj Mahal Casino is on the hotel's ground level. With the boardwalk and ocean just yards away, this cavern is free of natural light. Without a watch one wouldn't know the time, the day or even the season. There seem to be acres of gaming tables and slot machines. These machines can no longer aptly be called one-armed bandits since they are operated by the touch of a button, not by a vigorous pull on a lever. The arm is gone, but the machines remain bandits. Isn't this gaming invention a true triumph of business acumen? Watch a steady procession of middle- and lower-income men and women willingly, fearlessly, happily, tirelessly drop coins into a slot, pushing a button to make their money disappear. Go figure.

I spent just minutes walking through the Sands Casino (looking for a bathroom, if the truth be told, though there seems slim evidence that casino operators much favor truth). I dropped a quarter in one of the casino's slots and pushed the button. My coin disappeared in a whirl of wheels and was lost to me forever. I spent a few minutes more in the Taj, as they seem to call it. While there is no maharani buried there, plenty of dreams are deep-sixed daily. I lost another quarter after accidentally horning in on an older woman with dyed-black hair and silver sequins on her polyester top who had been playing two machines simultaneously. Had I won a barrage of silver coins, I would have feared her reaction.

A Judgment on All of Us

There is an enormous crystal chandelier hanging over The Donald's casino in a mirrored, gilt-framed vault. One can only imagine the horrific expense. Standing there among the few looking up, I felt suddenly and overwhelmingly sad for the pastors and pastoral committees who, seeking to improve worship and its environs, are greeted with the angry and even self-righteous cry, "This money should be spent on the poor." Indeed, more, much more, should be spent on the poor in this post-welfare age. But what of those fortunes lost to greedy entrepreneurs a dollar or five at a time, and social security checks given over freely 25 cents at a time? How much of what is lost belongs, in justice, to the poor?

Pope Paul VI, in his 1971 apostolic letter *Octogesima Adveniens*, notes that "it is up to the Christian communities to analyze with objectivity the situation which is proper to their own country, to shed on it the light of the Gospel's unalterable words and to draw principles of reflection, norms of judgment and directives for action from the social teaching of the church." He also observes: "If, beyond legal rules, there is really no deeper feeling of respect and service of others, then even equality before the law can serve as an alibi for flagrant discrimination, continued exploitation and actual contempt."

John the Baptist, standing to one side, calls out: "Let the one with two coats give to the one who has none. The one who has food should do the same" (Lk. 3:11).

A blighted Atlantic City, sporting 14 glittering casinos, with plans for seven more, stands as a judgment on me and my two lost quarters, and on all of us who have dumped cash into hungry machines while the ever-present poor stand hungry on the fringes.

MY HUSBAND'S SECRET ADDICTION

Brenda Braniff, as told to Bob Trebilcock

Brenda Braniff, a homemaker, tells the story of her husband Sam's addiction to gambling. In a matter of months, she maintains, Sam went from playing twenty-five-cent video poker games to partaking in ten-thousand-dollar gambling binges. The amount of time and money Sam invested in gambling depleted his savings, threatened his business, and nearly destroyed his marriage and family relationships, Braniff explains. However, after participating in a residential treatment program for compulsive gamblers and their spouses, the couple began recovering from the effects of Sam's addiction. Bob Trebilcock is a freelance journalist.

Editor's note: The names and some identifying details in this selection have been changed to protect privacy.

On a Friday evening in December 1994, I found myself getting dressed in a suite at the Luxor Las Vegas hotel. Sam, the man I would marry in 24 hours, was waiting downstairs in the casino while I changed for dinner.

Sam and I had known each other for only six months, but we had really clicked. We were both in our early 40s and divorced. Sam joked that he fell in love with me because we'd both gone to the University of Florida and were Gator fans. All I know is that from our first dinner together, I felt like I'd known him all my life. I loved his warmth, his sense of humor, his enthusiasm for life.

I went downstairs. "You're not going to believe this," he said, with a big puppy-dog grin. "I just put three dollars in the slot machine and won a thousand."

At the time, Sam's good fortune seemed like a promising omen for two people about to bet on a future together. I never for a moment suspected that in less than two years gambling would almost destroy our marriage.

A Life Most Would Envy

On Sunday, we returned to our home in the Atlanta suburbs. From the start, our married life seemed perfect. I have no children of my

Reprinted from "A Husband's Secret Addiction," an interview of Brenda Braniff by Bob Trebilcock, *Good Housekeeping*, June 1997, by permission.

own, and now I was part of a large, closeknit family. Sam is the oldest of six, and he has five children (three adult daughters from his first marriage, and a teenage daughter and son from his second). We had a life most people would envy: a lovely home, good jobs, and loyal friends. While Sam was busy with his insurance business, I was helping a friend open a chain of packaging stores. In our spare time, we played golf and tennis, and followed the Gators.

One day in February 1995, Sam came home late from work. He said he'd been with a client, which wasn't unusual. But he didn't call, and that was unlike him. Over dinner, he told me he'd had lunch at Charleston's, a restaurant-bar near his office that I thought was seedy.

"Why did you go there?" I asked.

"They have a great buffet," Sam said.

Over the next few months, Sam came home late more often. And I frequently found receipts from Charleston's in the basket where Sam leaves his wallet and charge slips. The buffet can't be that good, I thought to myself.

I wondered if he was having an affair. But we hadn't been married that long, and we were still very affectionate with one another. Deep down, I was sure he wasn't, but I knew something was wrong; I just couldn't figure out what.

The Beginnings of Trouble

One evening in May 1995, we had a date to meet at a restaurant for dinner with one of my old friends. Six o'clock came and went. I called Sam's office; he hadn't been back to work since lunch. We waited for two hours, then left. On the way home, I drove by Charleston's and spotted Sam's car in the parking lot.

At first, I couldn't find him in the noisy, crowded bar. Then I saw him in a corner by himself at a video poker machine.

"I can't believe you stood me up to spend your time in a dive like this," I screamed.

Sam looked up. His eyes were red, and he appeared totally shocked. "Brenda, I'm really, really sorry," he kept saying.

By the time we got home, I had cooled off, and Sam had thought of an excuse. He said he wanted to give me and my friend a chance to talk alone, and that he had lost track of the time. Besides, he hadn't spent that much. He was betting a quarter at a time and had lost maybe $20 or $30. "I feel really stupid," he said. "I promise I won't go back."

It was a lie. I later learned that Sam was betting $10 to $20 a hand, and gambling away as much as $200 a day. He started playing the video poker machines that day in February when he first came home late. He had bet a couple of dollars against a friend as a lark. Officially, there wasn't much to win. Gambling is illegal in Georgia, but some convenience stores and bars try to sidestep the law by paying off winnings with tickets redeemable for prizes.

Broken Promises

Sam went back for lunch a few days later and played again. And then again. Soon, Charleston's was the only place he went for lunch. As he spent more money on the machines, he learned that the bar paid off the winnings of good customers in cash. By late spring, Sam was a very good customer.

Sometimes he won, but his winnings only kept him at the machines longer. Hiding the losses wasn't hard. We maintained separate bank and investment accounts, and Sam kept his checkbook at the office. As long as the bills were being paid, I had no way of knowing how much he was losing.

For the next few weeks, Sam came home from work on time. In June 1995, his daughter Laura came to spend the summer with us before heading off to college. Sam had set aside Father's Day so they could spend it together. But that morning, he left early and didn't come back. When he finally showed up around dinnertime, he was defensive and edgy, completely out of character with the easygoing man I had married.

"Where were you?" Laura asked. "I waited all day."

"I had stuff to do," he snapped, then stormed out of the room. I followed him into the bedroom.

"What's gotten into you?" I asked.

"I was gambling," Sam blurted out. "It's Father's Day," he added, "I can do whatever I want."

In the year that I had known him, Sam's children were always his priority. "It's bad enough that you stood me up," I said, "but she's your daughter, and you let her down."

Sam looked away, then threw up his hands. "I know," he sighed. "I just felt like doing something for myself. I promise I won't do it again."

Once again I believed him. Between his business, which was booming, his children, and a new marriage, Sam had a lot on his plate. Maybe he just needs a diversion, I told myself. I even felt guilty for overreacting.

Gambling Addiction

The idea that Sam might be addicted to gambling never entered my mind. Even now, it's hard for me to imagine that anyone can become hooked in a mere four months. But an expert we later consulted, Valerie Lorenz, Ph.D., executive director of the Compulsive Gambling Center, Inc., in Baltimore, says that Sam's story is common. Life events, like a new marriage or putting a child through college, can be stressful, and gambling provides an easy escape or release from such pressures.

But for the spouses and children of compulsive gamblers, there is no escape. We live through our own hell of stress, lies, and uncertainty.

And the rest of that summer was hell. Laura and I would often sit up nights wondering when he would come home. Sam was distant and irritable, and we argued constantly. I couldn't help worrying that our fights drove him to gamble more.

By then, it was clear to both of us that Sam had a serious problem. At my urging, he attended Gamblers Anonymous meetings. They seemed to help for a few weeks, but then he began coming home later and later, and I realized that instead of going to the meetings, he was hitting the machines again.

Then in April 1996, during her spring recess, Sam took his youngest daughter, Karen, and some of her high school friends to Hilton Head, a beach resort community in South Carolina. When he came home, Sam handed me a letter detailing a week of binge gambling. He was too ashamed and embarrassed to tell me any other way. In all, he had lost more than $10,000.

I was appalled and frightened at how out of control he'd become. We spent the next several days canvassing hospitals and therapists in Atlanta for a treatment program that would admit him but none like that existed. And Sam kept gambling. One night, he didn't come home at all. The following day, his office called. He hadn't shown up for work either. I was frantic; Sam had never stayed out all night before.

When I discovered that he wasn't at Charleston's, I went looking for him at an illegal casino that he'd starting going to. I found his car parked next to a nondescript gray building with no windows and a metal door.

Inside, it was dark except for the light emanating from row after row of video machines. There was no one in the room except for the manager and Sam. He was unshaven and wearing the same clothes he'd worn when he left the house more than 24 hours earlier.

I pulled him outside and pointed to a big dumpster on the side of the building. "Why don't you just jump in and close the lid?" I told him. "That's where you are right now anyway."

"It's like I'm trying to kill myself," he said in a dazed voice. "You, my kids, the business. I love you all, and I'm just throwing it all away."

Falling Apart

At my request, Sam moved into a motel. When he dropped by to take care of some chores around the house, he looked pale and tired. He told me he wasn't gambling, but in my heart, I knew he was lying. Still, I put off filing for divorce.

A few weeks later, in June 1996, one of the therapists we had consulted called to tell me about the Compulsive Gambling Center, a residential treatment program in Baltimore. Sam's children and I confronted him on Father's Day. We told him that he was destroying himself. We asked him to enter the program—if not for his sake, then for ours.

"I'll go," Sam promised, "but I have some loose ends that I want to wrap up at work first."

It was another lie. I knew from the secretaries in Sam's office that he was rarely showing up for work. With their assistance, I went through Sam's financial records. He had drained an escrow account and withdrawn the equity in his life insurance policy and the policies he'd bought for his children. He had also sold some of his mutual funds and was beginning to tap his business accounts. In all, he had spent more than $150,000 over the last year.

I couldn't bear to watch Sam lose everything. I had just told him that our marriage was over, and about the same time, his office staff threatened to quit. A few days later, Laura told Sam she was going to withdraw from school in the fall: She had seen his records and realized he had gambled away her tuition money.

With his world falling apart, Sam finally agreed to get help. That afternoon, Laura and I saw him off at the airport.

"Please don't give up on me," Sam asked.

"Go get help," I told him. "And we'll see what happens."

I wasn't convinced he was serious about getting help, or that I even wanted him back. There had been so many lies and broken promises.

Sam called every day. With each conversation, he sounded more like the sweet man I had married. Two weeks later, I flew to Baltimore to participate in a program for spouses. When you live with a compulsive gambler, you get caught up in his addiction, worrying about where he is and what he might be doing. Therapy helped me realize that Sam's gambling wasn't my fault and that I wasn't alone.

Learning to Trust Again

A month later, Sam returned to Atlanta and we started our marriage over—with some significant changes. I now control the bank accounts and pay the bills. Sam gets a spending allowance, which is just enough for lunch and gas. While it sounds like a childish restriction, it's important to remember that money is to a gambler what booze is to an alcoholic.

But the most important change is that Sam can now talk openly with me about his fears and impulses to gamble again. That's when we go for a walk or out to eat to get his mind off the urge.

We also attend support group meetings. Sam goes to at least one Gamblers Anonymous meeting a week, sometimes more. Twice a month, I go to Gam-Anon meetings for family members and friends.

I have to admit that I held my breath the first time Sam was late coming home from work. Though Sam hasn't made a bet in about 11 months, I've learned at compulsive gambling is an addiction, and recovery, like alcoholism, is a day-to-day process. But I'm slowly learning to trust him again.

These days Sam is a much happier person. He's enthusiastic about life again and more appreciative of what he has. So am I. I think back to that weekend in Las Vegas when we vowed to make a future together. For a while, our marriage seemed like a gamble, but now it's become a sure thing.

CHAPTER 3

GAMBLING
AND SOCIETY

LEGALIZED GAMBLING HARMS SOCIETY

Blake Hurst

Gambling provides no societal benefits, argues Blake Hurst in the following selection. Casino and lottery proliferation has caused an increase in compulsive gambling, the author points out. Moreover, he maintains that the increasing number of casinos on riverboats and Indian reservations draws revenue away from nearby businesses and thereby damages the economies of surrounding communities. Hurst contends that gambling does not necessarily increase tourism to these communities as previously expected; instead, it encourages the local poor people to gamble away needed income. Gambling should be denounced as a vice that hurts the economy and undermines the value of hard work, he concludes. Hurst is a Missouri resident who writes often for the *American Enterprise*, a bimonthly conservative journal.

"When you play the Lottery, Iowa wins." That's the tag line on each advertisement for the Iowa lottery, and at least it's honest, if not particularly appealing. ("When you gamble at Trump's, Marla buys more furs" would not seem to be a good way for Donald to increase his handle.) Missouri's ads read, "You can't win if you don't play." Well, I guess that's true, but your chances are only marginally improved if you do play. The odds against winning a dollar in Missouri's Powerball game are 84 to one. The chances of winning the jackpot are 54 million to one. But over $400 million were spent in 1995 in Missouri on lottery tickets, so the advertisements must be effective. Nationally, close to $40 billion is now spent on lottery tickets each year, and the advertising campaigns costing upwards of $400 million that fuel those ticket purchases are a national scandal. Joshua Shenk points out in a 1995 article in the *Washington Monthly* that lottery advertisements are the only form of advertising not regulated by truth-in-advertising laws. Billboards in the poorest areas of Chicago read, "This could be your ticket out." Can you imagine the uproar if a private company embarked upon an advertising campaign that cynical?

The fear that somewhere, someone might be crossing a state line

Reprinted from Blake Hurst, "The Government as Gambling Partner," *The American Enterprise*, March/April 1996, by permission of *The American Enterprise*, a Washington, D.C.–based magazine of politics, business, and culture.

with money in his pocket has galvanized state legislators to compete with neighboring states by allowing more and more forms of gambling, usually beginning with the lottery, then moving toward more lucrative forms of wagering. As recently as 1988, only Nevada and Atlantic City allowed casino gambling. Today, 23 states have legalized casinos, and 70 Indian reservations are home to casino gambling. Casino gambling revenues nearly doubled from 1988 to 1994.

Riverboat Casinos and Indian Gaming

Iowa was the first state to legalize riverboat gambling. Proponents sold gambling as a way to solve the economic problems of Iowa's river communities. Gambling would be isolated on the river, and after all, weren't riverboat gamblers, with their handlebar mustaches and white straw hats, sort of romantic? As originally enacted, Iowa gamblers could only bet $200 per cruise, with a $5 limit per bet. Iowa dropped her betting limits soon after Illinois, Mississippi, Louisiana, and Missouri legalized riverboat gambling. The state of Mississippi has 23 casinos and gambling revenues in the state are greater than all other retail sales. Many "riverboats" don't cruise anymore. Harrah's riverboat in Kansas City isn't even on the river. Instead, the "boat" floats in a man-made pond. The cruises were originally intended to allow the states to regulate both the length of time spent gambling and the losses by gamblers, as well as to segregate gambling from nearby communities. But those regulations cost the states revenue and are in the process of being thrown overboard.

In 1988, Congress passed the Indian Gaming Regulatory Act. Today, over $6 billion is gambled at Native American casinos. Connecticut's Foxwood Casino, owned by the Pequot tribe, is the biggest casino in the Western Hemisphere, with $800 million wagered annually. The Indian Gaming Act allows states to negotiate what games are allowable and how the loot is to be split with the Indian tribes. Connecticut's negotiations resulted in a $135 million windfall for the state in 1994, with an expected $150 million in 1996. Not to be outdone, Massachusetts, Rhode Island, New Hampshire, and New York are looking for Indian tribes of their own. It doesn't take a very large tribe. Twenty years ago, only one Pequot grandmother was living where the casino is now located. In Minnesota, each of the 100-odd members of the Mdewakanton Dakota tribe receives an annual check for $450,000 from the profits of the tribe's Mystic Lake Casino. In the Midwest, gambling profits have forced the Sac-Fox tribe to draw up strict regulations governing the percentage of Indian blood that entitles prospective Native Americans to a cut of the gambling revenues.

The Effects of Riverboat Gambling

Larry Stobbs is mayor of St. Joseph, Missouri, a city that's home to one of Missouri's six riverboat casinos. The casino is profitable, but Stobbs is a little disgusted with the gamblers who come there. In fact, he insists that local businesses around the casino have not benefited from its presence: "People don't want to stay in a hotel that charges over $10 a night, because they want to spend all of their money at the casino."

Casino gambling has been sold as the answer to economic problems everywhere it has been tried. But casinos serve as a gigantic sump, sucking sales from surrounding businesses. Manny Lopez, for example, owns a restaurant in Kansas City, and his sales have dropped 30 percent since a riverboat opened nearby. In 1994, the Illinois Better Government Association surveyed 324 businesses near riverboats. Fifty-one percent reported no increase in sales from gambling-related customers, and 12 percent reported a decline in sales. Ronald Reno, in a report for Focus on the Family, writes that the *Chicago Tribune* polled 25 businesses after a riverboat casino opened near Aurora, Illinois. Only three of those businesses attributed an increase in sales to casino-related customers. Four businesses that had closed blamed their failure on problems caused by the casino.

University of Illinois economist Earl Grinols studied the effects of riverboat gambling and found that "the net effect of gambling was that roughly one job was lost for each gambling job created." People who spend money at a casino can't spend it at McDonald's, or the ballpark, or the amusement park. Gambling cannibalizes existing businesses, and the overall economic benefit to the economy is nil.

Problem Gamblers

Of course, if the competition for consumers' carefully budgeted entertainment dollars were the only issue at stake, the case against gambling would be harder to make. But not all gambling revenues come from folks who just want a night on the town. Estimates of the number of problem gamblers range from 2 percent of the adult population to over 10 percent, but their numbers clearly are large, and increasing with the advent of readily available legal gambling.

Dial 1-800-BETS-OFF and you can talk to the state of Iowa's gambling therapists. This number for a hot line for gambling addicts sometimes appears on our local radio station immediately after an ad for Powerball, the latest lottery game. No one seems the least bit uncomfortable with the juxtaposition. They should be. Calls to Iowa's hot line have increased by 60 percent since 1991. One of the around-the-clock counselors who answer the number earned her empathy the hard way: on the last hand of cards she played, she lost $65,000.

Maryland estimates that problem gamblers cost the state $1.5 billion annually, and the total indebtedness of pathological gamblers in Maryland is over $4 billion. University of Massachusetts professor Robert Goodman writes in the *Wilson Quarterly* that the societal costs imposed by each problem gambler are over $13,000, with some estimates running as high as $52,000 annually. Gamblers Anonymous estimates there are 6 to 10 million problem gamblers in the U.S.

John Kindt of the University of Illinois says that "current data show that when gambling activities are legalized, economies will be plagued with 100 percent to 550 percent increases in the numbers of addicted gamblers." Ronald Reno quotes from a survey of pathological gamblers that found that 75 percent of pathological gamblers have committed a felony to support their habit. Henry Lesieur, a criminal justice expert at Illinois State University, says that problem gamblers engage in $1.3 billion of insurance fraud yearly. Which is not surprising, as Lesieur also estimates that the average gambler with a problem has from $53,000 to $92,000 in gambling-related debts.

As Speaker, Bob Griffin had ruled the Missouri House of Representatives forever, but because of his association with the gambling industry, his tenure is now over. His influence peddling for gambling interests taxed the patience of Missouri's Attorney General, and Griffin is under investigation by a grand jury. Griffin sent a letter to Sahara Gaming Corp. soliciting a $16 million share of its proposed casino for a client of his. Griffin maintains he was only acting as a lawyer, and Sahara couldn't possibly have felt threatened by his position as Speaker of the Missouri House, with life or death power over gambling legislation. Elsewhere, according to Rep. Frank Wolf (R-Va.), four state senators in Louisiana are under FBI investigation for influence peddling involving the gambling industry. Seventeen South Carolina legislators were convicted in 1991 in a gambling-related FBI sting operation. Six Arizona legislators pled guilty to accepting bribes to ensure passage of a bill to legalize casino gambling.

Gambling interests also spend huge amounts in legal contributions to politicians. Former presidential candidate Bob Dole recently raised nearly a half-million dollars at a fundraiser hosted by the owner of Las Vegas's Mirage Resort. The Republican party received $1 million in direct contributions in the 1994 election cycle, and millions more were spent to ensure passage of pro-gambling referenda. In the 1992 election cycle, according to Roll Call, the Democrats led Republicans in fundraising from gambling interests, but casino owners, unlike their patrons, like to back winners.

In an attempt to cut out the middleman, three Indian tribes in Washington state recently backed a referendum to distribute 10 percent of gambling-related profits directly to each registered voter in the state. Each year voters might have received as much as $100 apiece. Though the initiative was defeated, whatever the proposal lacked in good taste, it made up in honesty.

The Poor Gamble More

Keno is legal in Nebraska. For the uninitiated, keno involves sitting in a large, well-lit room and watching numbers posted on television monitors hung around the wall. If the numbers you circle on your tablet with a crayon are the same as they appear on the screen, you win. Brownville, Nebraska, a town of about 300 people near my home, has a keno parlor. During a recent visit, I was struck by the overall shabbiness of the place. The walls were peeling, stuffing poked through the upholstery, the food we ordered was cold—and the place was packed.

I knew almost everybody there. The guy at the next table was the janitor when I was in high school. A retired checker from the local grocery store is obviously a regular, and the lady who used to work at the local doctor's office was there too. The woman at a nearby table is a farmer's wife from just down the road. The folks whom I saw at the keno parlor are representative of gamblers nationwide. A study from the University of Nebraska found that "those at or below the poverty rate spent 7 percent of their family income on gambling, while those with middle and upper incomes spent only 2 to 3 percent of their income on gambling." A New York study found that in one poor section of Buffalo, residents spent 7.4 percent of their household income on the state lottery. In some lower-income suburbs in Illinois, the average household spends nearly $100 a month on the lottery.

William Thompson, in a study of gamblers at Wisconsin casinos, found that nearly a third of gamblers had incomes less than $20,000 per year. Only 13 percent of gamblers earned more than $60,000. In Minnesota, where welfare recipients can receive their benefits electronically, ATMs inside casinos pay out over $400,000 in welfare benefits annually.

Atchison County, Missouri, where I live, is a small rural county with a population of just 7,000, yet sales of lottery tickets here are $700,000 annually, 2 percent of all retail sales in the county. We live just 80 miles from riverboat gambling in St. Joseph, and 90 miles from horse racing, dog racing, and casinos in Omaha, Nebraska, and Council Bluffs, Iowa. Gambling has become the most ubiquitous form of entertainment in the area. Though gambling was sold to our communities as a way to increase tourism and bring money in from outside the local area, Brownville, Nebraska, and St. Joseph, Missouri, are not tourist destinations. The people frequenting establishments in these places are my neighbors, and they are the ones who will be dialing 1-800-BETS-OFF.

Yet despite the willing clientele, there remains much disdain for gambling in the country. Communities in Colorado, Illinois, Massachusetts, Michigan, Rhode Island, Vermont, and other places turned down gambling in 1994. Statewide referenda to legalize casinos failed in four states. Clearly, the public is not as enamored with legalized gambling as the politicians who benefit from gambling revenues.

The Case Against Gambling

The economic case against gambling is clear. Gambling doesn't create economic wealth, but rather transfers wealth from existing businesses to those lucky or influential enough to receive gambling monopolies from the state. Gambling increases political corruption and crime, and is a strikingly regressive means of raising revenue. Gambling increases revenues to government, and supporters of legalized gambling are quick to quote the benefits to state coffers. But they never mention the costs of gambling. Platte County, Missouri, receives no funds other than property taxes from the riverboat casino within its boundaries. Developers associated with the casino interests are urging the county to reduce the property taxes that the casino would pay, and to dedicate these taxes to improving the roads leading to the casino. But Platte County must pay the costs of prosecuting the steadily increasing number of people who paper over gambling debts with bad checks. Bankruptcies in Iowa increased nearly 20 percent in 1995, despite a strong economy. Consumer credit counselors report that gambling plays a role in nearly a fifth of their caseload. Ten years ago, only 2 percent of credit problems were related to gambling. Clearly, the taxes that states receive from legalized gambling are only one side of the ledger.

"People would be gambling with or without the lottery," insisted a New York state lottery official recently. But during a typical evening there are ten TV commercials for the New York state lottery within a two-hour span. Either the $23 million that New York spends on lottery advertising is totally ineffective, in which case it should be stopped, or lottery officials in New York and elsewhere are lying when they say they don't create gambling that wouldn't otherwise take place.

I can say this: there weren't a lot of numbers runners here in Atchison County until the state of Missouri and the local grocery store got into the business. When the state removes the stigma from gambling by promoting it as a way to help education, people who have never gambled develop the habit. Governments may not be able to control vice, but surely they ought not encourage it. Yet that is exactly what they are now doing. As George Will summarizes, state sponsorship of lotteries and other gambling has changed the status of gambling in just one generation from "social disease to social policy."

When governments present riverboat casinos as economic development, they diminish those who build farms and factories. When states spend millions urging their citizens to play the lottery, they devalue the efforts of those who work hard and invest wisely. "The pot's 11 million, so I called in sick to work," goes Mary Chapin Carpenter's song "I Feel Lucky."

"The way to get rich is a jackpot, not a job. . . . The route to the top is a scratch-off ticket, not scratching for success. . . . Work, thrift, prudence—who needs them? Math is hard; circling numbers with a crayon is easy." Are these lessons we should be teaching our children? One of the most disturbing things about today's love affair with the quick buck is what it says about the moral sturdiness of democratic government in the late twentieth century.

LEGALIZED GAMBLING IS PRODUCTIVE AND RATIONAL

David Ramsay Steele

In response to what he terms the nationwide "War on Gambling," David Ramsay Steele contends that legalized gambling is productive and should continue to be permitted by law. Claims that gambling enterprises hurt nearby businesses and foster compulsive activity are based on the exaggerations and faulty logic of gambling prohibitionists, Steele asserts. He maintains that most gamblers behave responsibly, make rational decisions, and do not overestimate their chances of winning. Steele is the author of *From Marx to Mises: Post-Capitalist Society and the Challenge of Economic Calculation* and the coauthor of *Three Minute Therapy: Change Your Thinking, Change Your Life*.

The War on Gambling is about to take its place alongside the War on Drugs as a crusade for decency which no ambitious politician may question. The present movement to legalize gambling, which got under way in the 1960s, is still making some gains, but has become increasingly unpopular. The momentum of legalization has been slowed, and will soon be reversed. Although some gambling is now legal in all but two states (Hawaii and Utah), gambling prohibitionists are confidently predicting absolute nationwide prohibition by early in the twenty-first century, and it's by no means self-evident that they are wrong.

Government policy on gambling has gone through successive cycles of liberalization, backlash, and renewed prohibition. In the U.S., we are currently experiencing the third nationwide backlash—the first was in the middle of the nineteenth century, the second during the 1940s.

The ease with which public opinion can be mobilized against gambling reflects a deep-rooted suspicion. Most people enjoy gambling in moderation, and will gamble occasionally if they can. Yet these same people often oppose further liberalization of the gambling laws. Gambling is one of those things which are obviously harmless when you or I do them, but fraught with menace if millions of other people can do them too.

Reprinted from David Ramsay Steele, "Yes, Gambling Is Productive and Rational," *Liberty* magazine, September 1997, by permission of Liberty Publishing.

Why Is Gambling Denounced?

Why is gambling, enjoyed by the vast majority of people, denounced day in and day out, with hardly any voices to be heard in its defense? The reigning ideology tells us all that gambling is evil, for several reasons. Gambling is selfish; it is addictive; it provides "false hope"; it is a dangerous competitor to some forms of religion because it too offers the prospect of a greatly improved future life at rather long odds.

Yet possibly the single most influential reason for holding gambling to be evil is the belief that it is unproductive and therefore wasteful. Today's hostility to gambling has much in common with the old opposition to "usury" (charging interest on loans) and the current fear of "deindustrialization" (replacement of manufacturing by service jobs). Money-lending, hamburger-flipping, and playing the lottery have all been maligned as essentially sterile pursuits whose expansion bodes ill for the health of the nation.

Is gambling unproductive? We need to distinguish between the more or less remote *effects* of gambling and its *intrinsic nature*. It is sometimes claimed that gambling encourages people to dream impossible dreams about the future instead of working hard, or that gambling encourages crime at the expense of honest industry. Aside from these alleged effects of gambling, however, it is commonly believed that gambling is intrinsically unproductive—that in gambling, unlike farming or auto manufacture, nothing is produced.

Sterile Transfers of Money?

Claims about the injurious *effects* of gambling don't seem to be factually correct. Freedom to gamble encourages hard work on the part of gamblers, especially those with low incomes, just as, broadly speaking, any enhanced opportunity to spend one's earnings as one pleases increases the incentive effect of a given wage. And gambling by itself does not attract crime: it is the illegality of some or all gambling which forces gambling to become a criminal activity.

Is gambling, then, *intrinsically* unproductive? One very popular view was promulgated by Paul Samuelson in his once-canonical textbook: gambling "involves *simply sterile transfers of money or goods* between individuals, creating no new money or goods." A footnote informs the reader that "in all professional gambling arrangements, the participants lose out on balance. The leakage comes from the fact that the odds are always rigged in favor of the 'house,' so that even an 'honest' house will win in the long run." Notice the nasty quotes around "honest," and the use of the word "rigged" to represent the fact that these sneaky casino operators do not provide their services as a charity, but require to be recompensed for their efforts, just like college professors or writers of textbooks.

Before we look at the claim that gambling involves nothing but sterile transfers of money or goods, let's first consider a related charge levelled by anti-gambling propagandists. One of their leaders, Robert Goodman, contends that gambling, when it is permitted after a period of prohibition, displaces or, as he picturesquely terms it, "cannibalizes" other activities.

Goodman continually reiterates this charge, and doesn't seem to notice that it applies equally to any activity which consumes scarce resources—any activity whatsoever. If pizza restaurants were first prohibited and then legalized, the newly legal restaurants would attract some dollars away from other businesses. Buildings, kitchen equipment, tables, delivery vehicles, and employees would be bid away from other kinds of restaurants, and perhaps some resources would be bid away from non-restaurant activities, to cater to the consumers' newly-liberated demand for pizzas. One might then observe that pizza provision grows only by hurting other occupations—that pizzerias "cannibalize" other trades.

If, after being prohibited, a casino is permitted to open, this may well cause people to spend in the casino some money they would formerly have spent in a restaurant. Perhaps that restaurant has to close because of reduced business. Precisely the same would apply in reverse: if casinos were legal, but restaurants prohibited, and then restaurants were legalized, the newly legal restaurants would attract consumers' dollars away from casinos, and some casinos might have to close. Anti-restaurant fanatics could then proclaim that restaurateurs were nothing more than dastardly cannibals, gobbling up legitimate businesses such as casinos.

When a heretofore prohibited but widely desired activity is legalized, the expansion of this activity will necessarily curtail other activities, unless total output increases. This does not mean that the change is unimportant. The fact that people pursue the newly legal activity demonstrates that there is an unsatisfied appetite for that activity. The people who desire to take part in the prohibited activity, and are now free to do so, experience an improvement in their situation, in their own judgment. Their real incomes automatically rise, even though this increase is not captured in national income statistics.

There are two important qualifications to what I have just stated. First, the legalization of a formerly prohibited industry reduces the demand for other industries below what it would otherwise have been, not necessarily below what it has actually been. If total output rises—if there is economic growth—casinos may attract business from restaurants, and yet restaurants may keep the same business as before, or even expand. Second, prohibition of gambling does not succeed in stopping gambling. While prohibition reduces the total amount of gambling, some gambling goes on illicitly. A major part of the expansion of legal gambling following legalization takes away business from formerly illegal gambling rather than from non-gambling activities. . . .

The fundamental argument for legalizing gambling is not that it will bring in business from elsewhere, but rather that people are entitled to do whatever they please with their own lives as long as they don't invade other people's rights. More generally, it is good for people to be free to do what they want to do, so long as this does not impose on anyone else.

One reason why the "cannibalization" argument is so often made is that many people start with the prejudice that gambling is a waste. If gambling is unproductive, and if the growth of gambling subtracts from some productive activity, then this must, it seems, be bad. But if it is bad for gambling to cannibalize restaurants, yet okay for bookstores to cannibalize drycleaners or for churches to cannibalize bowling alleys, then cannibalization is not what is really being objected to. We come back to the inherent legitimacy of gambling, and the dominant view of that is mightily influenced by the popular theory that gambling is necessarily unproductive.

Production Means Satisfaction of Wants

What does it mean to say that some activity is unproductive? This question was picked over quite thoroughly by economists in the eighteenth and nineteenth centuries. One early view was that only agriculture was productive. Manufacturing (then a small part of total employment) was looked upon as unproductive, since it was obviously supported by agriculture—the manufacturers had to eat. Another idea was that only products which could be turned into gold and silver were truly productive. Later these two theories lost any serious following, but two others remained popular for a while: that anything which did not result in a new physical object was unproductive, and that what we would now call "service" jobs were unproductive. (These two views are not the same, and do not necessarily mesh together well, for a provider of services, such as an architect, may assist in the creation of a new physical object, such as a house.)

Adam Smith contended in 1776 that the labor of domestic servants, government officials, the military, "churchmen, lawyers, physicians, men of letters of all kinds; players, buffoons, musicians, opera-singers, opera-dancers, &c." were unproductive. This contention, and the sloppy argument of which it forms a part, provoked much debate over the next century.

The attempt, by Smith and others, to designate some occupations as unproductive did not lead to convincing conclusions. Those who based productiveness on the making of a physical object were compelled to conclude, for instance, that the performance at a musical concert would be unproductive, whereas printing the tickets and programs for that same concert would be productive.

After the end of the nineteenth century, leading economists no longer paid much attention to the classification of activities as productive or unproductive. The new theory of value based on marginal utility shone a flood of light on the question, and clearly exposed many of the old arguments as fallacious.

The conclusion of the new approach was that "production" means satisfaction of wants. It is productive to make a physical object only insofar as that object enables someone to satisfy a desire. In satisfying desires, the physical object (such as a shirt) yields services. All production is ultimately production of *services* desired by consumers. The musician giving a live performance is being directly productive in the only way in which it is intelligible to be productive: he is satisfying the wants of consumers, in this case of listeners. The producer of a shirt is being productive more indirectly, by making an object which will yield a stream of future want-satisfactions to its wearer. If for some reason the shirt cannot yield these want-satisfactions, whether because everyone undergoes a conversion to an anti-shirt religion or because the shirt falls apart before it can be worn, then the labor of producing it has turned out to be unproductive, despite the fact that a physical object was made.

One way of describing want-satisfaction is to talk about "utility." An activity is productive if it yields utility. According to the modern view, which is no longer controversial among economic theorists, domestic servants, entertainers, priests, and physicians are indeed productive, because they produce services their customers want; they enable those customers to get additional utility.

The same applies to activities in which people may engage either individually or collaboratively. It is productive for a musician to give a recital, assuming that the audience likes it, but it is also productive for a group of friends to get together and perform music for their own enjoyment, or for an individual to perform alone for his own satisfaction.

"Productive" is not a value-judgment. If gambling turned out to be productive, that would not show that we would have to approve of it, but it would show that if we disapproved of it, we would have to do so on grounds other than its unproductiveness.

Does gambling satisfy the wants of its participants? Do gamblers enjoy gambling? If they do, then gambling is productive, in much the same way that sports, religious services, or psychotherapy are productive. . . .

Are Lotteries Productive?

Many people will readily agree that if a concert, a baseball match, or an evening's conversation are considered productive, a poker game might also be judged productive. But there is another kind of gambling: playing the lottery. Surely this can't be primarily an enjoyable way to pass the time. It seems to be done in hope of financial gain, but what if that hope is a product of delusion?

An activity may be anticipated to be productive, but found not to be productive after the fact. Drilling for oil may be unproductive if no oil is found. Technical terms sometimes used for such a distinction are *ex ante* (looking forward before the outcome) and *ex post* (looking backward after the outcome). The anti-gambling ideologue may say: Granted that gambling is productive *ex ante*, it is most often unproductive *ex post*.

Normally we would expect a person to learn from his mistakes, to give up futile endeavors and turn his attention to more successful avenues. Therefore, the mere fact that someone persists with some activity strongly suggests that this activity is productive for that person. It is claimed, however, that the gambler is unable to learn from experience. He is like a driller for oil who keeps coming up dry, but repeatedly pours money into an endless series of unsuccessful drills. Because of a flaw in his thinking, he is unable to learn from experience, despite the fact that he doesn't get what he pays for. Is playing the lottery inescapably irrational? If it is, then lottery playing may perhaps be considered unproductive *ex post*.

Anti-gambling dogmatists usually hold a distinctive interpretation of the motivation for gambling. They maintain that gambling occurs because individuals seek monetary gain, that this desire for monetary gain must be disappointed in most cases, and that therefore the persistence of gambling is irrational—either stupid or involuntary. It is often contended (or just assumed) that a rational person would never gamble. Gambling, on this interpretation, occurs only because gamblers fail to understand elementary probability theory, or, understanding it, cannot bring themselves to act upon it. The cliché that lotteries are "a voluntary tax on the stupid" echoes Sir William Petty (1623–1687), who argued for state management of lotteries on the grounds that the state already had the care of lunatics and idiots.

Gambling prohibitionists are always falling over themselves to "explain" . . . that "gamblers must lose in the long run," that "the odds are stacked against the gambler," that "gamblers as a whole can only lose," and so forth. They pronounce these marvelous insights as though they were gems of wisdom which gamblers must have overlooked. And perhaps a tiny minority of gamblers have indeed missed these earth-shaking commonplaces—after all, people have been known to make silly mistakes in all departments of life, from music to marriage, so there's no reason why gambling should be immune. But I can't see any evidence that the general run of gamblers behave irrationally, or that they would stop gambling if they took a course in probability theory.

Gamblers Do Not Over-Rate Their Chances

On the most straightforward level the lottery player gets precisely what he pays for: an equal chance with other players of netting a very large sum of money, of becoming rich. The anti-gambling ideologue, however, will press the point: objectively, the lottery player gets exactly what he pays for, but he is unable to evaluate it correctly, so he never gets what he believes he pays for. He does not appreciate how slim are his chances of becoming rich. His intuitive notion of his chance of winning is unrealistically high because of a peculiar mental defect.

How does the anti-gambling preacher know that the lottery player over-rates his chances? Why don't we suppose that, on average, the player rates his chances exactly correctly? Anti-gambling zealots reply that he then would never play the lottery! This argument is fatally circular and therefore worthless. Although anti-gambling zealots often insinuate that rational people would not gamble, there exists no serious argument for any such assumption.

The claim that the gambler overestimates his chances is usually asserted as a blind dogma, with no evidence offered. However, some anti-gambling propagandists mention, as though it were significant, the fact that the whole class of lottery players must lose on balance. In technical terms, playing the lottery is not a "fair" bet; the "expected value" of a lottery ticket is below the price of the ticket.

The expenses of organizing a lottery have to be covered out of sales of tickets. Therefore, the amount returned in prizes is lower than the amount paid for tickets. A technically "fair" lottery would be one in which the total prize money were equal to the total money paid for tickets. In such a lottery, what is called the "expected value" of a ticket would be the same as the ticket price. It is an error to suppose that this offers a criterion of rationality: that it must be irrational to play the lottery when the expected value is below the ticket price. That any such supposition is faulty can be seen upon a moment's reflection.

The proportion of total ticket revenues returned in prizes from lotteries is commonly around 60 percent, though it is sometimes more than 70 percent, and with some of the new state lotteries is little more than 50 percent. If lotteries were purely private and open to competition, this figure would immediately rise to well over 90 percent (except where particular lotteries were openly allied with charitable donation), but it could never reach 100 percent without the lottery's making a loss. Just suppose, however, that a lottery were subsidized, so that 105 percent of the prize money were returned in prizes. Would it then become rational always to buy lottery tickets, and irrational to fail to do so? If so, how many tickets? How much of one's income would it be obligatory, if one were rational, to allocate to lottery tickets? Suppose now that the lottery were hugely subsidized, so that, say, five times the ticket revenues were returned in prizes (but most entrants would still win nothing), what then? At what point, as we increased the subsidy to the lottery, would it become incumbent upon any rational person to buy a ticket?

A Matter of Personal Preference

There is no such point—though there would empirically be a point where the majority of people, or the majority of people with math degrees, would judge that one would have to be a lunatic not to buy at least one ticket. This kind of thing is a matter of personal preference, a matter of one's personality and worldview. It is "subjective" in the sense that there is no single demonstrably correct answer for any rational agent. Such judgments can be influenced by miscalculations or other mistakes, but if all mistakes were eliminated, there would remain a diversity of preferences. Given these preferences, one's behavior is also affected by objective circumstances like one's income.

A lottery player will usually prefer a lottery which returns 90 percent of the ticket revenues to one which returns only 80 percent. Therefore, some will be induced to play at 90 percent who would not play at 80 percent. But someone who plays the lottery buys a chance of being in for a big win, and there is no justification for the assumption that the individual's valuation of this chance, the amount of utility he derives from being aware of it, has to coincide with the "expected value" of a lottery ticket (the prize money multiplied by the chance of winning). There are many cases where it clearly ought not to do so (for example, if the price of a ticket is one's entire income for the next few weeks, so that one will die of starvation unless one wins the prize, it would not be sensible to enter with a one-in-a-million chance of winning, even if the prize were so heavily subsidized that the expected value of a ticket were a thousand times the ticket price).

A rational person doesn't have to value a one-in-a-million chance of getting a million dollars at precisely one dollar. You may value such a chance at one cent or at five dollars—either way (though this may tell us something about your personality) there's nothing wrong with you. However, assume for a moment that the "expected value" theory of rational gambling were correct. Suppose that you paid a dollar for a ticket giving you one chance in a million of winning $700,000, with $300,000 of ticket sales going to run the lottery and pay off the state. The expected value of your one-dollar ticket would be 70 cents. Only 30 cents would have to be explained by non-pecuniary elements (a sense of participation, giving something to a good cause, and so forth, or, if we want to indulge in flights of fancy, by "irrational compulsion" or "enhanced daydreaming"). It would follow that at least 70 cents out of each and every dollar spent on lottery tickets would indisputably be rationally allocated. Is this better or worse than the dollars spent on furniture or books? Casual discussion of the rationality of buying a ticket often tacitly assumes that "expected value" is the rule, but then proceeds as though the entire sum spent on tickets would be shown to be irrationally spent, when in fact (on the erroneous assumption that expected value should fix the buyer's valuation of a ticket) only something less than half of the ticket price would then, arguably, be spent irrationally.

The fact that a lottery is not technically "fair" follows automatically from the fact that the costs of running the lottery have to be covered out of ticket sales, and is otherwise a complete red herring from which no conclusions about the rationality of the players may legitimately be drawn. It's a feature of any system for re-allocating existing endowments, such as a subscription to the March of Dimes: organizing a subscription costs something, so the total paid to beneficiaries must be less than the total contributed. This is ineluctable, and in no way sinister. A lottery is simply a way in which a lot of people each put in a small sum, and then a few of those people picked at random get large sums. Nothing in the world could possibly be more harmless or more innocent than this.

Is Insurance Irrational?

Insurance is a negative lottery. In buying insurance, we pay a small sum now to guard against the low probability of losing a large sum in the future, just as, with a lottery, we pay a small sum now to engineer a low probability of winning a large sum in the future. Insurance is always an unfair bet—much less fair than a competitively run lottery, because the costs of running an insurance company greatly exceed the costs of administering a lottery.

Do the ideologues who berate gamblers for their irrational short-sightedness also berate those who, for example, insure the contents of their houses against fire? Quite the contrary! This willingness to pay for insurance more (sometimes vastly more) than its "expected value" is lauded to the skies as the epitome of responsible behavior. *Failure* to take *this* unfair bet is commonly considered thoroughly foolish and even irrational. In the debate over Hillary Clinton's health care plan, it was generally considered a self-evident scandal that an appreciable number of young, fit, comparatively high-income people chose not to buy health insurance, such a scandal that it warranted their being *compelled* to buy it—forced to make this extremely "unfair" bet.

What goes for insurance goes also for precautionary outlays of a non-pecuniary kind, like wearing a car seat belt or getting a polio shot. In a typical recent diatribe against gambling, totally bereft of any serious thought and seething with the malignant compulsion to control other people's lives, one Robyn Gearey blasts the New York state lottery because, *inter alia,* the odds of winning a big prize are less than the odds of being struck by lightning. Aside from the question of whether this is factually correct, Gearey evidently believes that being struck by lightning is a negligibly unlikely event which shouldn't influence a rational person's plans, yet my guess is that Gearey does not inveigh with comparable enthusiasm against the installation of lightning rods.

Lottery Players Are Rational

Some months ago, a thousand-pound man was in the news. He had lain on his bed for years; his main physical exercise was calling the local deli to send round a few dozen sandwiches at a time. The medics had to knock down a wall to get him out of his house and carry him to the hospital.

It would not be sensible, in a discussion of whether to let individuals decide for themselves what to eat, to keep bringing up the case of this thousand-pound monster. Similarly, it would not be appropriate, in a discussion of whether to permit people to attend a church of their own choosing, to endlessly pontificate about the Heaven's Gate suicides.

Yet just such irrelevance is the normal practice with anti-gambling bigots, who compulsively prattle on and on about problem gamblers, people who gamble away their life savings and desert their families for the gaming tables. Such cases are a tiny proportion of gamblers, and most of the people who behave like this would behave just as badly if gambling did not exist. Typically, and overwhelmingly, gamblers practice strict self-discipline and moderation. If they are on low incomes and play the lottery regularly, they often spend less than the price of a six-pack per week. Any freedom of any sort affords the opportunity for foolish behavior by a foolish minority, and that exceptional behavior can never justify clamping iron shackles on the overwhelming majority of people who are sensible and self-disciplined.

The allegation that gamblers are irrational can be tested. We can look at their behavior for signs of irrationality. In all respects which I have seen reported, the vast majority of lottery players behave as if they were rational. They prefer games where the odds are better. (Everyone understands that, to maintain a viable state lottery, private lotteries have to be outlawed.) They bet only a small amount per week. When they win a big prize and become rich, they husband their winnings prudently.

People play the lottery more if they have few other options with lottery-like qualities: the stock market, venture capitalism, an exciting career, a songwriting avocation. Young, talented people with few commitments have many such options, and will respond rationally by playing the lottery rarely. A 55-year-old janitor with ten kids and no equity has hardly any options, and will respond rationally by playing the lottery more frequently. This is just what we observe; it fully corroborates the rationality of playing the lottery. Lottery tickets are the janitor's cattle futures. To blame him for playing the lottery is like reproaching him for not having the good taste to drive a Ferrari.

Lottery players seem to understand the odds quite well (unlike the anti-gambling lobbyists, who demonstrate their innumeracy every time they open their mouths); the players certainly do understand with perfect clarity that it is far more likely than not that if they play every week of their lives they will never win a big prize. They still think it is worth playing, and it is just ignorance to imagine that this judgment of theirs must rest upon a miscalculation. Lottery players hold that it is better to have played and lost than never to have played at all. Who is to say that they are wrong?

Casinos Have Proven Beneficial to Deadwood, South Dakota

William V. Ackerman

William V. Ackerman discusses the results of his research on the effects of gambling on Deadwood, South Dakota. According to Ackerman, casinos, which became legal in Deadwood in 1989, have boosted revenues from recreation and tourism and have revitalized the local economy. Gambling operations in Deadwood created eighteen hundred new jobs in the area, the author points out, and casino profits paid for the renovation and preservation of the town's historic buildings. Although escalating real estate values and property taxes have been somewhat of a burden on residents and nongambling establishments, Ackerman concludes that for the most part casinos have made Deadwood a better place to live. Ackerman is an assistant professor in the department of geography at the Lima campus of Ohio State University.

Population and economic activity continue to decline in small towns and cities in many rural areas of both the United States and Canada. Maintaining essential retail and service businesses and adequate infrastructure are issues of concern to community residents and public officials in declining places. Both historic preservation and legalized gambling have been suggested as potential remedies to this continuing decline for some communities.

I conducted on-site research in Deadwood, SD, during the summers of 1994 and 1995 to compile a case study of the effectiveness of legalized gambling in generating sufficient economic activity to revitalize a declining city and provide the monetary resources for historic preservation. Through interviews with local officials and reading of government reports, I found that gaming receipts and resultant tax revenues continue to increase in Deadwood despite widespread legalization of gambling elsewhere. The city is working on the traffic congestion and parking problems caused by increased tourism. And many residents remain committed to using the positive aspects of gaming to maintain the city's new-found vitality.

Deadwood, the Lawrence County seat, is a small community of

Reprinted from William V. Ackerman, "Deadwood, South Dakota—Gambling, Historic Preservation, and Economic Revitalization," *Rural Development Perspectives*, Summer 1996, courtesy of the author.

approximately 2,000 persons located at the bottom of a narrow gulch in the Black Hills of South Dakota. The city limits are severely constricted by topography and National Forest boundaries. Interstate Highway 90 is within 9 miles of Deadwood, connecting it to Rapid City, the largest town in the area, and points beyond.

Deadwood began with the gold rush to the Black Hills during the summer of 1875. Deadwood's economy progressed in a series of booms and busts, each new boom a function of new mining or milling technology that revived profitable mining in the area. Gold-mining continues today at the Homestake mine located in nearby Lead, approximately 3 miles south of Deadwood.

Over the years, Deadwood developed a colorful and exciting history. The city was notorious for prostitution, gambling, and opium dens and boasted of such famous residents as Wild Bill Hickok and Calamity Jane. From its inception, Deadwood was a business center for the Black Hills mining region, and for generations it was the legal, mercantile, entertainment, railroad, and financial center of an immense area of the West.

Changes in transportation technology during the 1930's and 1940's caused Deadwood to lose its importance as a wholesale center. Businesses in Rapid City, more centrally located for both shipping and distribution of goods by truck, increasingly took over wholesale functions for the Black Hills region. Since the 1960's, Deadwood's retail prominence was lost as a result of I-90 bypassing the town, competition from a large regional mall in Rapid City, and the recent location of K-Mart and WalMart stores in nearby Spearfish.

As wholesale and retail activities declined, Deadwood was supported primarily by tourism. Tourism provided a living for a number of store owners and employees, but the activity was highly seasonal and did not provide adequate income to support major infrastructure improvements. City population fell from 3,045 in 1960 to 1,830 in 1990, and many retail outlets closed as a result of the eroding customer base.

The Need for Historic Preservation

Deadwood's designation as a National Historic landmark makes preservation particularly important. By the mid-1980's, however, deferred maintenance threatened many of the city's historic buildings, and the National Trust for Historic Preservation placed the entire city on their list of endangered sites. In 1989, estimates of the cost to meet the historic preservation goals of the city ran between $20 and $60 million.

Throughout the 1970's and 1980's, concerned local citizens and government officials had been searching for resources to save the historically significant, but decaying, infrastructure. However, traditional attempts to attract new businesses to Deadwood failed. Some of Deadwood's citizens refused to give up and in 1986 formed the "Deadwood U Bet" organization. This group advocated legalizing limited stakes gaming to generate additional tourist trade and to provide a source of funds to protect, revitalize, and restore the city. This initiative gained momentum when, in 1987, a fire destroyed an important segment of the historic downtown and awakened citizens and the State government to the real peril facing the community.

To sanction legalized gambling in Deadwood, the committee had to overcome several obstacles: (1) the constitution of South Dakota had to be amended to permit gambling, (2) the State legislature had to approve the measure, and (3) Deadwood voters had to approve by a majority of at least 60 percent. All of these requirements were successfully met, and legalized gaming officially began at high noon on November 1, 1989.

Gambling Spurred Local Growth

Deadwood's decision to use legalized gambling to revitalize and preserve their historic community was unique. At its inception, only Nevada and Atlantic City, New Jersey, had legalized gambling; no other small community in the United States had tried such a solution to community revitalization and preservation.

The effect of gaming was large and immediate. In the first 8 months, a total of $145.4 million was wagered in Deadwood, almost 73 times the amount the South Dakota Commission on Gaming had projected. Within a short time, 84 casinos were operating in Deadwood. Gaming activity in Deadwood has continued to increase despite fast-growing competition from other States. By 1994, 10 States allowed casino gaming, 25 others had tribal gambling, and approximately 2 dozen casino riverboats were active on the Mississippi River and the gulf coast. An estimated 70 percent of the U.S. population currently lives within 300 miles of a casino.

Each fiscal year from 1990 through 1995 has seen Deadwood's gaming activity increase and generate increasing revenues for the city, county, and State. In total, gaming generated taxes and fees of $43.4 million during its first 6 years. Deadwood has received over half of these revenues for historic preservation activities.

The State has received $5.2 million for operating expenses of the Commission on Gaming, $1.7 million for the State Tourism Promotion Fund, and $5 million for general use. Lawrence County has received $1.6 million, and $100,000 has been dedicated for historic preservation projects in other parts of South Dakota.

The tax revenues accruing to Deadwood are held by the City of Deadwood and administered by the Deadwood Historic Preservation Commission. The Commission has allocated these funds to provide for preservation of the built environment and to upgrade infrastructure to support the historic architectural resources. Projects have included (1) restoring and repairing public buildings and infrastructure, (2) improving visitor services, parking, and transit, (3) providing for adequate city planning and historic preservation supervision, (4) assisting the Deadwood Visitors Bureau in marketing programs, (5) funding low-interest loans for restoration of historic commercial and residential properties and grants to nonprofit organizations to restore historic buildings, (6) providing interpretive materials for historic walking tours and related programs, (7) funding the legal costs of historic preservation projects, and (8) providing professional archeological and engineering studies for private and public projects.

In addition to the tax receipts that have reverted to Deadwood, substantial private investment has been made in the city to refurbish historic buildings for use as gambling casinos. The dual requirements of historic preservation and commercial building codes have led owners to restore, to as great a degree as possible, the original Victorian Era appearance of their buildings and to bring their buildings up to code, including installation of sprinkler systems to limit the potential of major fires. The expected cost of improvements listed on building permits from 1990 through August 1994, the period of peak renovation, totaled $26.8 million. The actual cost of improvements is generally higher than that estimated on building permits. In Deadwood, the actual cost of improvements was underestimated by 70 to 100 percent. Based on these figures, the private sector spent between $34.8 and $53.6 million on restoration through August 1994. The combined private/public sector investment in Deadwood from the approval of gaming through 1994 has amounted to between $64.1 and $82.8 million.

The improved business activity and higher property values in Deadwood also generated increased sales and property tax revenues for the city, county, and local school district. In 1989, Deadwood's total city budget was $1,596,400. The city's 1995 budget was $11,102,900. The need for city services also increased over the period, but the revenue increase is estimated to be over twice as fast as the increase in service needs. The major portion of the budget increase in Deadwood has come from gaming taxes and has been allocated to historic preservation, public works, and public safety. Lawrence County gained $1.5 million in property tax revenues due to the increased value of Deadwood real estate, plus an additional $1.6 million as their share of gaming taxes. These monies have been allocated to a number of projects used for general improvement in county services. The Lead-Deadwood school district budget increased from $4.9 to $6.1 million between 1989 and 1995. During the same period, school enrollment dropped by 25 students from 1,467 to 1,442, and school personnel increased by 5, from 177 to 182. Most of the increased revenue was used to raise the salaries and fringe benefits of teachers and support staff.

Through employment of workers, gaming has affected an even

wider area. An employment survey I conducted in August 1994 recorded place of residence for the employees of all but one casino, a small operation that employed fewer than 10 persons. Total surveyed employment was 1,796 persons, not counting owners/managers. Of those, 33.2 percent lived in Deadwood, 27.6 percent in Lead, 19.2 percent in Spearfish, 7 percent in Sturgis, 6.5 percent in Rapid City, and 3.3 percent in Belle Fourche. An additional 3.2 percent commuted from various small towns around the Black Hills, including Newcastle and Upton, WY.

A wage survey by the Deadwood Gaming Association in March 1994 found that gaming employees were paid an average annual wage of $13,494 without tips. Most workers indicated that they earn good tip income, so assuming a tip of 15 percent on top of their annual wage boosts their estimated annual earnings to $15,519. Multiplying this estimate by the number of gaming employees in 1994 produces an estimate of $27.9 million of income directly generated by gaming. . . .

Legalized gambling provided badly needed jobs and funds for economic revitalization and historic preservation. However, gaming dramatically changed the business functions in Deadwood. With the onset of gambling, approximately three-fourths of the businesses on the historic Main Street became casinos. Deadwood lost businesses offering new car sales, ladies' clothing, ladies' shoes, and appliances, along with the town's only department store and its only furniture store. Given the depressed pre-gaming economic climate of Deadwood, many of these businesses were already struggling to survive and many likely would have been forced to close even if the casinos had not opened. Other small towns in Saskatchewan and the Northwestern United States have lost population and business functions without gaining replacement businesses.

Many landowners, seeing the opportunity for increased profits, quickly turned existing businesses into gambling enterprises; others sold to investors at prices 4 to 10 times previous appraised values. Some elected to lease to gambling operations, and a few continued to operate their original businesses without gaming devices.

Most Casinos Have Started Showing Profits

While the casinos were viewed by many as an opportunity for increased profits, Deadwood's gaming establishments, on average, did not show a profit until 1992. During 1992–94, casinos reported an average profit of 4.9 percent, with 62 percent of them reporting profits and 38 percent reporting losses. Currently, three casinos in the historic district are closed. With a third unprofitable and a few closed, can gaming sustain long-term growth and historic preservation in Deadwood?

Casino profit margins are limited by State-mandated payouts. State law currently requires that a minimum of 80 percent of gaming receipts be returned to the bettors. Casinos can return more if they choose, and since the inception of gaming the average payout to players in Deadwood has averaged 90 percent. Profits are also related to the volume of players, location of the casino, business skills of owners and managers, taxes, licensing fees, and many other factors. In Deadwood, casino profit margins are significantly affected by taxes. In addition to the State and Federal taxes all businesses pay, each gaming establishment is required to pay an annual licensing fee of $2,000 per device (slot machine, gaming table), and each casino is allowed a maximum of 30 devices. In addition, casinos pay an 8-percent tax on revenues. Between Fiscal Year (FY) 1990 and FY 1995, the licensing fee plus the revenue tax combined to generate an average tax of 18.5 percent of operating revenue. The licensing fee, being a regressive tax, affects low-volume operators most, reaching an effective tax rate of 50 percent of operating revenue for some operations.

In any line of business, a certain amount of failure is the norm, especially during the first few years of operation. The failure of a business in Deadwood, however, may be a concern because it creates a vacant building. Excessive vacancy could damage the city's image and add to the difficulty of protecting the historic environment.

Traffic and Property Tax Problems

Gaming has generated two other problems for Deadwood that need to be resolved: (1) traffic congestion and scarce parking, and (2) rapidly rising property taxes. An additional concern . . . that gaming would greatly increase crime in the community has proved unfounded.

The number of visitors to Deadwood increased by two to three times following the legalization of gaming, reaching an estimated 1.5 to 2.0 million visitors annually. This increase generated an immediate need to provide adequate parking and to minimize peak-period traffic congestion. Visitors surveyed during 1991 and 1992 cited lack of adequate parking as their most frequent problem. Parking problems are expected to further intensify as current building projects will double Deadwood's lodging capacity from 600 to 1,200 rooms.

Peripheral parking development is limited by Deadwood's location in a narrow canyon surrounded by the Black Hills National Forest. Changing the built environment of the city to accommodate additional streets and parking is constrained by its historic landmark status. In 1995, Deadwood officials were granted funds by the Historic Preservation Commission and the Business Improvement District to develop plans for a 375-space multi-level parking structure to be located off the main street near the city center. The bonding for this project has been approved and construction [began] after Labor Day 1996. The town, in cooperation with the Dunbar Corporation, has also developed an imaginative approach to solving the traffic and parking problem, while adding to the historic flavor of the region.

They propose to rebuild an abandoned rail link from the small city of Whitewood, approximately 9 miles north of Deadwood and situated on I-90. This project will allow parking for large numbers of automobiles near the Whitewood station and provide visitors a scenic rail trip to Deadwood. Part of the restoration is currently out for bid, and the Northern Hills Railroad Authority is setting up a bond issue for the balance of the project. Operation is optimistically expected to begin in 1998.

Rapidly escalating property values and taxes are a burden on Deadwood residents and businesses alike and impede progress toward Deadwood's goal to diversify the economy. New, nongaming businesses are unlikely to locate in Deadwood given the high cost of land and the existing tax structure. The assessed value of property within the city increased from $25.9 million in 1990 to $87.6 million in 1994, a jump of 338 percent over 4 years. The assessed value of commercial property has increased by 527.9 percent, the value of residential property has increased 166.2 percent. The increased tax generated annually by the change in valuation exceeded $2 million in 1994.

Property taxes have increased the most on commercial property in the gaming district where real estate values have escalated dramatically. In 1990, the average assessed value for main street businesses was $37,442. By 1994, that average had increased to $451,772, an increase of more than 1,200 percent. The average annual property tax bill has increased from $1,225 to $14,777. Perhaps the most inequitable impact from increased property tax affects those businesses in the gaming district that have chosen not to become gambling establishments. For example, a hardware store that benefits very little from tourist trade experienced an increase in annual property taxes of $10,114. Under a 1977 South Dakota law, the cost of historic preservation work can be deducted from the appraised value of the property for a period of 8 years. While this helps some property owners finance restoration, it does not protect against increased valuation based on escalating real estate values.

Most Residents Are Hopeful

Although not all Deadwood residents are comfortable with the changes in their community, the majority are proud of the restoration that has taken place and do not want to return to pre-gaming economic problems. Rather, their vision for Deadwood involves using the positive aspects of gaming to make the city a better place to live.

Total gaming receipts and resultant tax revenues continue to increase despite widespread legalization of gambling across the United States. The city is working on its traffic congestion and parking problems. If casino closures or increasing property taxes become too burdensome to sustaining the local economy, the city, county, and State governments and the citizens who worked to bring legalized gambling to Deadwood will undoubtedly work to solve those problems as well.

Deadwood appears to enjoy a situational advantage over many competitors. The city is located in the scenic Black Hills, is near Mount Rushmore, has an exciting history of gold and gunfighters, and combines all this with legalized gaming. Such a mixture appears to provide a solid base for continued economic success.

Casinos Have Ruined Deadwood, South Dakota

Elizabeth Manning

Deadwood, South Dakota, has lost its Wild West, mining-town charm since the introduction of gambling establishments in 1989, contends Elizabeth Manning in the following selection. She points out that the rapid proliferation of casinos in Deadwood resulted in an increase in rents and taxes and forced small retailers to shut down. Deadwood has also witnessed an upsurge in traffic congestion and crime, Manning maintains, and many of the town's residents lament the loss of community that has accompanied the gambling boom. Manning is a former staff reporter for the *High Country News*, a biweekly journal that focuses on environmental issues.

Before state residents legalized gambling in Deadwood, South Dakota, in 1989, most people in this town of 1,800 or so lived life in the slow lane. They'd see each other for coffee at Marie's Cafe or later in the day at Olé's for a game of cards. Except for a few hundred jobs provided by the Homestake Gold Mine, the town scraped by on seasonal tourism. Summer provided the biggest boost, when thousands of bikers rolled into town for the annual Sturgis Motorcycle Classic and Rally, the second-largest biker gathering in the nation.

But above all, people visited Deadwood in the Black Hills because it was part of the Wild West. This is the mining camp, founded in 1876, where Wild Bill Hickok was shot. He'd only been in town a few weeks when he made the fatal mistake of sitting with his back to the door, playing a poker hand of black aces and eights, known thereafter as a Dead Man's Hand. This was also home to Calamity Jane, Poker Alice, Preacher Smith and Potato Creek Johnny, a beloved, 4-foot-3-inch prospector from Wales who found one of the Black Hills' biggest gold nuggets. Less well-known figures had nicknames like Jimmy-Behind-the-Deuce, Bummer Dan and Slippery Sam.

Legal or not, some bars offered poker games and "for amusement only" slot machines. The upstairs still housed prostitutes. This rough-and-tumble legacy lingered until the 1980s, when state and federal

Reprinted from Elizabeth Manning, "Deadwood Pays Dearly for Gambling Riches," *High Country News*, April 1, 1996, with permission.

agents shut down the last three whorehouses and many retailers closed their doors. Deadwood was almost dead, and a new Wal-Mart and Kmart in nearby Spearfish promised to put the final nail in the coffin.

"We were left with about 10 shops that sold rubber tomahawks nine months out of the year and were boarded up the other three," says Mike Trucano, who owns Black Hills Novelty, a slot and game machine business.

An Economic Shot in the Arm

Then town leaders hit on an idea: Why not legalize some gambling and turn Deadwood into a year-round tourist town? This would bring back the flavor and fun that had left with the madams. Tax revenue from gaming would help prop up the crumbling buildings and replace outdated water and sewer lines.

The goal wasn't to recreate Las Vegas, but rather to supply an economic shot in the arm. There would be mini-casinos offering poker, blackjack and slot machines with $5 bet limits at establishments such as the Old Style Saloon No. 10, said to be where Wild Bill was shot. To open a casino, businesses would also have to run another non-gambling enterprise such as a restaurant, bar or soda fountain. Town leaders proposed a limited number of machines for each building; the first suggestion was 15, later upped to 30. Gambling would act as a magnet to draw in tourists. But, the thinking went, the town itself, and the beauty of the Black Hills, would keep them coming back.

Trucano and seven other locals formed a committee called "Deadwood, You Bet" to promote the idea. They crisscrossed the state drumming up support for a state constitutional amendment legalizing limited gambling inside the city limits of Deadwood. The signature drive worked: It went to the ballot and passed in November 1988, by 64 percent; the state legislature passed enabling legislation in April of the next year; and finally, Deadwood citizens approved gambling in a special town election. The new gambling era began at high noon on Nov. 1, 1989.

The change was dramatic: Deadwood went from boarded-up to booming almost overnight. Streets and sidewalks were ripped up to restore the cobblestones and to put in new water mains. The city renovated its fire station, museum and library. City hall and the police station moved into new digs, and a visitors' center was opened in the old train station. The improvements were underwritten with bonds the city is paying back with gambling taxes. And the money flooded in: Some 2 million tourists spent $150 million in Deadwood in 1995. Of that, the city collected roughly $5 million in gaming taxes.

Bad News for Locals

But amid all the new money, the locals lost control.

Since 1989, Deadwood's gaming halls have multiplied, going from nine at the start to a current high of 80. Today the town has 2,242 slot machines and 68 blackjack and poker tables. Every Tom, Dick and Jane opened a casino, and the governor-appointed South Dakota Gaming Commission let them.

It approved casinos whose only retail was a T-shirt or candy stand. By loosely defining what a "building" was, some casinos were allowed to put in more than 30 machines. Based on the original architecture, the foundation plan or the number of businesses, the gaming commission might decide a single structure should be counted as two or three buildings. The Gold Mine resort, a new hotel in the planning stages, is bending the law creatively: Its foundation is split into 13 foundations, enough "buildings" for 390 slot machines.

Betty Whittington, a Deadwood, You Bet member who has since changed her campaign buttons to read "Deadwood For Sale," says town leaders might have put the brakes on the explosive growth. "But it would have taken someone with backbone." She says the gambling commission and carpetbaggers that moved in forgot that there was a town—and townspeople—here at all.

Now, the people of Deadwood are split on whether their new-found prosperity is worth it. A few have moved away in disgust. Others, like Mayor Barbara Allen, believe it was a matter of survival: "We have a degree of confidence now that we'll still be here tomorrow," she says.

But gambling has exacted a price: When the people of Deadwood lost control as casinos proliferated in their town, they also lost control of their rents, their taxes, their mobility and their community.

Deadwood's Stalemate

There's a phenomenon scholars call "cannibalization" that often occurs when gambling is introduced in a free-market economy. Real estate speculation drives prices sky high on Main Street; many businesses willingly sell out to the first buyer. Then as casinos rake in cash hand over fist, the hold-outs soon sell or convert to a casino.

Before gambling there were nine stores in downtown Deadwood, including three car dealerships, a department store, a few clothing shops and an auto-parts store, points out Susan Kightlinger, a former Chamber of Commerce employee. There wasn't much to cannibalize, and within a year, they were all gone. Virtually no retail exists in downtown Deadwood today—and there are definitely no gathering spots like Marie's Cafe.

Hilda Fredericksen, who raised six children in Deadwood, misses the old bowling alley the most. Now, it's Deadwood Gulch Resort, with a casino and an 8,000-square-foot arcade—Gulches of Fun—for kids.

Cannibalization has extended to the casinos themselves, as some, especially the smaller ones, are finding it hard to make a living in such a competitive world. Deadwood enjoyed a brief monopoly when gambling first became legal, but three mining towns in Colorado and scores of Indian reservations have since opened up casinos of their own. In addition, state-operated video-lottery machines greet South Dakotans in nearly every pizza parlor, bar and liquor store. Having bought in at inflated prices, Deadwood casino owners find it almost impossible to sell.

Today, it seems more like a stalemate than a boom.

Deadwood's state of limbo is apparent at the Fairmont Hotel. A brothel in boom times and a flophouse during busts, it's now a casino. Owner Ron Russo has put $1.6 million of his own money, plus $300,000 in historic preservation loans from the city, into the hotel. He keeps the casino open but says his hotel still needs about $1 million in improvements. The downstairs is mostly restored to its historic glory; the upstairs remains stuck in the flophouse days.

Russo, a former cable TV executive with a New Jersey accent, is eccentric enough to fit in with Deadwood's past. Usually wearing a leather vest, he looks like a biker who came to the Sturgis Rally and never left. He can talk for hours about his plans for the hotel, or about the junk he's found while renovating: suitcases belonging to the bums who once slept here and old gaming tables hidden during a big raid in the 1940s. Downstairs, in the basement, he shows off the bar where he hosts parties for the bikers in August; the countertop is recycled from one of Deadwood's defunct bowling lanes.

He wishes he had the money to finish the hotel, but he still hasn't paid the previous year's taxes. He hopes to pay them soon—and get back the wine license the city suspended—when he sells some property to the city.

Russo believes real estate will rebound when Deadwood becomes more a destination resort. He says he'll probably sell the hotel then, because "it gets hard seeing people lose their money gambling."

Growing Pains

Casino owners aren't the only ones with economic troubles. Residents like Hilda Fredericksen and her husband, Dwayne, moved from a house downtown to Deadwood's only mobile-home park, Claim Jumpers, when casino traffic made parking too difficult. She took that move in stride—after all, she had seen other area residents relocated for expansions in mining, which was Deadwood's mainstay industry before gambling. But now Claim Jumpers has a new owner who raised the rents by $100, and rumor has it he might build a motel or casino there. The Fredericksens may have to move again.

Property owners are also being hit. Gambling proponents promised property taxes would go down because of casino profits. Instead, taxes have gone up all over the state. Elmer Pritchard, a city commissioner and owner of the town's Laundromat, says his slot machines don't make him any real money. "It just about pays my property tax," he says.

Although Deadwood residents say they still feel safe, crime has increased nearly three-fold since gambling—and its attendant growth and tourism—began. And despite the enormous amount of money flowing through the town, Lucile Tracy, who runs a program called the Lord's Cupboard for the Methodist church in nearby Lead, says she hands out food to about 200 people a month, compared to three people a week before gambling arrived. Some of those people are compulsive gamblers, but many are newcomers who come to work in the casinos at $4.25 an hour, and find it difficult to feed their families and pay the bills.

"It's real hard for me to condemn the casinos, though, because they bring in big vanloads of food," says Tracy.

A Deal with the Devil

Some residents say all the other growing pains pale in comparison to the loss of community. They feel they forfeited their downtown in a Faustian trade for survival. Hilda Fredericksen says it's a standing joke: "Gee whiz, we have to go to Sturgis, Spearfish or Rapid City to see someone you know from Deadwood."

Kids complain they have nothing to do. Since most casinos don't allow minors, they say the only remaining hang-outs are the fast food joints.

Some people say it's even taken the fun out of gambling. Before legalization, people used to make sure problem gamblers didn't get in too deep, says Whittington. It wasn't unusual for a bar owner to return money to customers who lost too much. Now it's too corporate and state regulators wouldn't allow it. "I'd rather deal with the Mafia than get picked to death by bureaucrats," says Whittington.

Though it's difficult to imagine amid the din of slot machines, some people predict Deadwood will become South Dakota's Aspen—a once-funky mining town transformed by big bucks and newcomers into a resort for the rich and famous.

Mayor Allen says town leaders are trying to avoid "Aspenization" by bringing back a sense of community. The town hopes to build a regulation-size ballfield and spruce up the rodeo grounds.

Some residents say the town's only choice is to get bigger and better. In gambling, it's called chasing your losses.

Enter Kevin Costner, the Hollywood actor, and his brother Dan. Costner rediscovered the Black Hills during the filming of *Dances With Wolves*. Shortly after gambling became legal, he and his brother bought the Midnight Star, which they turned into the classiest casino and restaurant in Deadwood.

Now they're planning a resort and casino, scheduled to open in May 1998, that should transform the town yet again. The new resort will be called the Dunbar, after John Dunbar, the character Costner played in *Dances With Wolves*. With 838 acres and 320 rooms decorated Ralph Lauren Western-style, it promises to be a hotel the likes of which the Wild West has never seen. Plans include an 18-hole golf course, tennis courts, an equestrian center, a fishing lake, a snow bowl for sledding, a full gym, and of course, the casino. Jim Fisher, program director for the resort, says costs will likely exceed $100 million.

The Dunbar will cater to a whole new corporate clientele, says Fisher. Resort planners are hoping to lure urban professionals from both coasts and from abroad—especially from Japan, where people are crazy about Kevin Costner and the Wild West. Rooms will go for $200 and up in the summer, Fisher says.

Townspeople have heard the rest before: They won't come just for gambling. They will come for conventions, to ski at one of the two local resorts or simply to enjoy the beauty of the Black Hills.

Fits and Starts

But it's been rough going for the Costners, slow enough to make some locals wonder whether it will really happen.

First, a land trade between the Costners and the Forest Service angered a few vocal Lakota Sioux, one of the tribes that had befriended Costner during the movie filming. The Sioux have long fought for land rights in the Black Hills, and some were angered by the brothers' plans to build a resort on land they consider theirs.

Then the Costners said they wouldn't build their resort unless the state raised the bet limit from $5 to $100. After three separate votes in the state legislature, the bet limit narrowly passed, only to be defeated in a statewide referendum that anti-gambling forces in South Dakota campaigned to put on the ballot.

After the last defeat, the Costners threatened to pull the plug on the project. So the state, the county and the town of Deadwood offered the brothers millions in tax breaks, plus help with a short-line railroad between Rapid City and Deadwood. The railroad and steam trains will be paid for by state bonds but guaranteed by the Dunbar.

Now that the resort seems to be chugging full-steam ahead, the town is preparing itself for the new breed of tourist and looking forward to the better-paying jobs the Dunbar will offer. Residents are hoping some retail businesses will return, though they realize the stores are more likely to be J. Crew than J.C. Penney.

Most town residents think of the Costners as "Deadwood's great white hope" (though they've been called a few choicer names as well).

Town leaders say even if the project fails, they still need to keep upgrading what they offer tourists. "To me, the Dunbar is always icing on the cake," says Franklin Hotel and casino owner Bill Walsh, a former priest who gave up the Catholic church for "the theology of leisure." "We're already a destination resort town."

Mississippi Monte Carlo: Gambling and Race Relations in Tunica County

Benjamin Schwarz and Christina Schwarz

In 1990, when gambling was first permitted along the Mississippi River, officials in Tunica County, Mississippi, hoped that casinos would provide employment opportunities for the area's poor black majority. Instead, authors Benjamin Schwarz and Christina Schwarz report, the casinos created an economic prosperity that appears to be drawing affluent whites into the area's planned housing developments. Meanwhile, they maintain, Tunica's poorly educated blacks have not been able to take advantage of casino employment opportunities and, faced with rising rents, are under financial pressure to leave. Benjamin Schwarz is a senior fellow at the World Policy Institute in New York. Christina Schwarz is a fiction writer.

Tunica County, Mississippi, was notorious as the poorest county in the poorest state in the country even before 1985, when Jesse Jackson declared that he had found "America's Ethiopia" there. Life for Tunica's black majority started out hard and got no easier, as statistics from the 1980s testify. The county recorded America's eighth highest infant-mortality rate, the fourth highest percentage of births to teenage mothers, the highest percentage of people living below the poverty line, and the lowest median household income. In 1984, 70 percent of residents over the age of twenty-five had no high school diploma. Nearly a quarter of the houses lacked modern plumbing. The filthy tin-and-wood shacks that disgusted Jackson rotted along "Sugar Ditch" Alley, named for the open sewer that ran through it. Such infamy inspired a few federal housing projects, but in 1992 the county was still a symbol of rural poverty. Tunica's unemployment levels were among the highest in Mississippi, and many of those who had jobs did not make enough money to get off welfare. That year more than half the county relied on food stamps.

In 1986 the best that the governor, Bill Allain, could hope for in

Reprinted from Benjamin Schwarz and Christina Schwarz, "Mississippi Monte Carlo," *The Atlantic Monthly*, January 1996, by permission of the authors.

Tunica was that "a little industry" might "come in there and employ fifty, a hundred, or two hundred people" in minimum-wage jobs, but even that seemed highly unlikely. Tunica, on old two-lane Highway 61 at the northern tip of the Mississippi Delta, was so isolated, and its population so miserably educated, that even state monetary incentives and federal tax breaks could not entice business. Despite the sign outside the county seat that declared Tunica A GOOD PLACE TO LIVE, many parents who wanted a decent life for their children encouraged them to leave. Waiting for opportunity to come to Tunica was futile.

Hope for Tunica County

Or so it seemed. Today there is light in Tunica's future. The highway along which Tunicans once migrated north in search of jobs now glows with billboards and searchlights luring 1.2 million visitors a month into the Delta. At the hamlet of Robinsonville a brand-new four-lane access road under a canopy of sodium lights draws drivers west toward the banks of the Mississippi River, where an Irish castle, a Wild West town, a Tudor mansion, a circus tent, a plantation house, a Hollywood studio, and an enormous western saloon—casinos all—float in a sea of parked cars. Their marquees promise shows by Ray Charles, Johnny Cash, and Tanya Tucker. A few feet from these spangled façades dark acres of cotton and soybeans spread under the Delta night, silent except for the bullfrogs and the mosquitoes. Entering the casino lots feels like stepping out of real life.

"Can you believe this?" one woman asks another, as they shuffle forward, waiting at midnight for a table in a casino restaurant. "Right in the middle of the cotton fields," she marvels.

No one dreamed that casino gambling would take off the way it has in Tunica, says Ken Murphree, Tunica County's administrator. But the county that for decades could attract no industry has turned out to be an ideal location for the casino trade.

In part this is because Mississippi is eager to accommodate gaming. The state collects only eight percent of its casinos' revenue—among the lowest tax rates on casino gambling in the country and less than half the rate that neighboring Louisiana assesses. Moreover, Mississippi charges a casino only $5,000 every two years to renew its license, whereas Louisiana charges $100,000 every year. While most other states restrict the number of casinos and their concentration, Mississippi models itself on Nevada, the king of the gambling states, granting an unlimited number of licenses and letting the market alone decide which and how many of the fledgling casinos will survive.

They are allowed plenty of leeway to compete. Mississippi's casinos, unlike those in many other states, may devote as much floor space as they please to gambling and may install as many gaming tables and slot machines as they want to fill. While some states try to legislate against gamblers' tendency toward excess by forbidding bets over $5.00, Mississippi, like New Jersey and Nevada, lets its gamblers play for high stakes.

Ironically, Tunica's poverty helped to determine the county's success as a casino mecca, because it made Tunicans receptive to the notion of legalized gambling. Throughout the nation casinos have mushroomed in areas that have despaired of other sources of income. Tunica fits the pattern. When, in 1990, the state authorized casinos along the Mississippi River and the Gulf of Mexico, Tunica was the first county on the river to welcome the industry. "We weren't smarter than other areas," Murphree is fond of saying. "We were more desperate.". . .

Hitting the Jackpot?

In some ways Tunica has hit the jackpot. Observing the astonishing success of the first casinos, the county, which gets four percent of casino revenues, hoped eventually to see an increase in its budget from $2.8 million to $7 million. In fact by 1995 the county budget had shot up tenfold, to $28 million. Tunica's poor black population has also benefited from the casinos. Since gambling was legalized, the percentage of county residents receiving food stamps has fallen from more than 50 percent to 37 percent, and the county's collection of child-support payments has jumped from under $40,000 to between $60,000 and $70,000 a month.

Nevertheless, the casinos have not rescued Tunica's poor. Although with eight casinos the county of 8,300 people now has more jobs than residents, most of those jobs, particularly the better-paying ones, have gone to people from outside the county. And whereas boosters claim that the casinos have dramatically reduced unemployment, in fact the average unemployment rate for October of 1994 through September of 1995 was 14.5 percent—only slightly lower than the average rate of 15.1 percent for 1991, the year before the first casino opened. In September 1995 unemployment was 13.6 percent, about twice the average rate in Mississippi as a whole. Only three of the state's eighty-two counties now suffer greater unemployment than Tunica. In the face of persistent unemployment, those who are well-off continue to insist that "there is a job for everyone who wants one"; but their emphasis has begun to fall on the second clause, so that an observation that once seemed to express relief and celebration now suggests exasperation and disgust. One woman we talked to expressed this bluntly, complaining, "You could put a factory in some people's back yard and they still wouldn't work."

Derrick Crawford, the county's director of human services, finds this view unfair. He points out that one kind of employer cannot possibly suit every potential employee, and that for religious reasons alone many of Tunica's blacks would rather be unemployed than work in a casino. Still, like many others, he ultimately lays the blame on what is most often called the "lack of work ethic"—meaning that many Tunicans make poor employees because they haven't been con-

ditioned to take a job seriously. People hint that those who are continually out of work are in that situation because they come to work
late, take unauthorized days off, or even quit on a whim. Crawford
and others see Tunica's history of unemployment as responsible for
this behavior. "If you're twenty-six or twenty-seven and never had a
job," Crawford says, "nothing has taught you how to work."

A Crippled Black Population

In 1989 the Lower Mississippi Delta Development Commission,
chaired by Bill Clinton as the governor of Arkansas, issued a more
sweeping statement about the limitations that cripple the black population in Tunica and other Delta communities: "By any objective economic, educational or social measurement, the . . . people in the
Delta region are the least prepared to participate in and contribute to
the nation's effort to succeed in the world economy." Most Tunicans
are simply unable to take advantage of the new opportunities that the
casinos have brought to their doorstep.

The disparity between the way most Americans live and the way
the majority of black Tunicans live defies belief. With the exception
of crack cocaine and, now, the casinos, little of modern America has
penetrated Tunica County; far from participating in the American
dream, most of Tunica's black population is excluded from even the
mundane aspects of American life.

"This is a different world," Dorothy Rhea, a waitress at one of the
casinos, says, describing the sensation of coming to Tunica from
Memphis, Tennessee. To explain what she means, she tells a story of
working with a new waitress, a young black woman from Tunica.
"She's holding out a plate of bacon," Rhea says of the other woman,
"and she keeps asking me, 'Is this toast? I need toast. Is this toast?'"
The woman was not being sarcastic, Rhea explains. "She really didn't
know what toast was."

But the county's problems are even more complex than its grim
statistics and such examples of isolation from America's mainstream
would suggest. "Race," as one woman told us, "is at the heart of
everything here in Tunica."

Blatant Separation

Not everyone is poor in what has sometimes been known as the poorest county in America. Pointing out the big landowners, Tunicans
often claim that the county is home to more than thirty millionaires.
Perhaps more important, Tunica, unlike most rural counties in the
South, has almost no poor whites. In fact, in the county seat, the
town of Tunica, which is 74 percent white, the county's reputation for
poverty is difficult to credit. The wide main street is lined with a few
basic shops—a hardware store, a drugstore, two banks—and is refresh-
ingly free of links from any fast-food chain. An old-fashioned brick

courthouse stands in the middle of town. Some of the houses in the most visible neighborhood are modest, though solid and well tended, but most are substantial, and a few might be called mansions. All sit back from the street on large, leafy lots.

To be poor in Tunica County is to be black. Most blacks live outside the town limits—the county as a whole is 74 percent black and only 26 percent white, the reverse of the town. Many blacks live in North Tunica, better known as the "sub" (short for "subdivision"), an unincorporated area adjacent to the county seat. There is some federally subsidized housing in the sub—small, neat brick ranch houses, trailers, and an apartment complex that looks like a barracks. And there are many houses that might more accurately be called shacks. No white people live in North Tunica, and the town has no desire to annex it. . . .

The blatant separation of the races in Tunica's schools shocks an outsider even more than the county's housing pattern, and neither blacks nor whites seem to object to this separation, which is most shocking of all. With few exceptions, Tunica's white children attend the private, all-white Tunica Institute of Learning. White churches reportedly raise funds to help the small number of white families who otherwise could not pay the tuition. Tunica's black children go to the public schools. In 1995 only one white student attended Rosa Fort, the public high school. Significantly, he was not from Tunica; his family had just moved into the county from California.

Certainly Tunica has changed radically since the 1940s, when the county sheriff accused the folklorist Alan Lomax of being a foreign spy because he violated the county's racial code. Lomax was detained because he interviewed the blues musician Son House, a black man, without permission from the planter for whom House worked, because he referred to House with the honorific "Mister," and because the sheriff suspected that Lomax had shaken House's hand. Today the sheriff of Tunica County is black. But while Tunicans now eschew the virulent racism of the past, the attitude that fueled the old behavior—what scholars generally agree comes down to a fear of miscegenation—has merely been tempered, not eradicated. The principal of Rosa Fort, Willie Dismuke, who is black, is surprisingly offhand, for instance, when he mentions that fear of interracial dating is at the heart of the separation between the schools. A racial code still dictates relations between whites and blacks in Tunica, constricting both groups. As Sister Gus Griffin, of Catholic Social Services, a social-service organization in Tunica, observes, "I think in the social structure of Tunica white people would be ostracized if they sent their kids to Rosa Fort. Whites are in line too. They're not free."

Race relations influence Tunica's response to its new wealth, and in this way the county's plans for its future are the inevitable flowering of its history. Tunica has shared that history, for the most part, with the rest of the Mississippi Delta. . . .

"The Most Southern Place on Earth"

The historian James C. Cobb, perhaps the leading authority on the region, has called the Mississippi Delta "the most southern place on earth." Its history is the history of the South at its most extreme. From the start the Delta presented an opportunity for high-stakes gambling. The soil promised quick riches in cotton, but those who tried to win them risked cholera, malaria, and typhoid fever, and climatic extremes ranging from drought to floods to frost. Those whose bodies survived the diseases and whose crops survived the weather could see the whole endeavor come to nothing in the fickle cotton market. Such a gamble attracted wealthy landowners from the East whose plantations were wearing out and who could afford the enormous investment in cash and slaves necessary to clear and drain and cultivate the land. Producing a profitable cotton crop in the Delta required physical labor above all. By 1850 the slaves on whom the planters depended for this labor outnumbered whites in the most developed area of the Delta by more than fourteen to one.

Black men and women transformed the Delta. As writer David Cohn explained, without the African-American there would be no Delta as we know it today.

> The Negro's identification with the life of the Delta is fundamental and complete. . . . It was he who brought order out of a primeval wilderness, felling the trees, digging the ditches and draining the swamps. The vast rampart on the levees upon whose existence the life of the Delta depends sprang from the sweat and brawn of the Negro. Wherever one looks in this land, whatever one sees that is the work of man, was erected by the toiling, straining bodies of the blacks.

With its grueling, year-round work, malarial swamps, and planter class frantic to see its gamble pay off, the Mississippi Delta was perhaps the worst place in America to be a slave. Being "sold down the river" to the Delta quickly developed a reputation as a death sentence. At the other extreme the members of the Delta's white elite, freely spending their profits in dissipation and ostentation, soon became known for their pursuit of the good life. Poor and middle-class whites had no place in this plantation economy. "By the middle of the nineteenth century," Cobb writes, "the Delta had already assumed an enduring identity as a region where a wealthy, pleasure-seeking, and status-conscious white elite exploited the labor of a large and thoroughly subjugated black majority."

Long after the Civil War whites remained convinced that their success depended on the Delta's being a place where their interests, solely because of their race, always came first. As one Tunica County planter told a sharecropper early in the twentieth century, "This is a place for me to make a profit, not you."

Race Relations in the Delta

However subjugated, blacks were essential in the Delta, since the cotton plantations continued to require a large labor force. Delta whites thus had to coexist with a group they feared but on whom they depended, and this, along with a bedrock of racial animosity, underlay the relationship between the races for decades. Beginning in the late 1940s, when cotton production was mechanized, eliminating the need for most agricultural labor, this relationship changed fundamentally. "By the end of the 1960s," Cobb maintains, "Delta blacks [were] largely superfluous to the economic interests of Delta whites"—a situation that largely defines race relations in the Delta today.

Although mechanization spurred a huge black migration to the North—part of the largest population movement in American history—African-Americans still make up nearly 70 percent of the Delta's population. The paramount problem in Tunica, from the point of view of many whites, is what to do with this group that stayed behind—a black majority disproportionately unemployed, dependent, and miserably educated, a population that many whites regard as dross. In fact, the wish of some whites, one white woman from Tunica whispered to us recently, "is for [black people] to go away," leaving Tunica for the whites. For both political and economic reasons, this has been true since mechanization. The black population, for its part, seems pretty well convinced that its fortunes in Tunica will never change. This resignation gives rise to a resentful passivity, which the white population perceives as an unwillingness or inability on the part of blacks to improve their situation. The behavior of each side thus confirms the worst suspicions of the other.

Prosperity for Some

Tunica is really two communities, deeply divided by race and wealth, and the economic boom that was at first greeted as a universal good has in many ways exacerbated the county's division. Blacks believe that even if casino revenues prove to be a rising tide that lifts all boats, it still won't lift them out of their subordinate position. Some blacks fear that Tunica's new prosperity might make their place in the county even more marginal.

Whereas legalized gambling is the most recent in a series of attempts to bring industry to the area, historically such efforts have been designed to retain and increase the minority white population rather than to create employment for blacks. Many of Tunica's whites, it seems, see casino gambling as a means to transform Tunica into a white middle-class exurb of Memphis.

Ken Murphree, the county administrator, talks hopefully about golf courses, factory-outlet malls, and retirement communities to solidify Tunica's new image as a center for recreation and leisure. His wife,

Connie Murphree, points out that Tunica's quiet rural atmosphere would make it a haven for those who want to escape urban problems. If the casinos succeed, and the leisure industry develops as its boosters hope, the county will attract young couples wanting to work and retirees ready to play, and will house them in new condominiums and planned communities. Eventually Tunica will attract middle-class families with jobs in Memphis who want a better house on more land than they can afford in the city, and the county, with what its promoters call a "nice little Southern town" at its core, will prosper as a bedroom community for Memphis and a retirement center for the mid-South.

Tunica's blacks are conspicuously absent from this vision. In fact, it's impossible to reconcile the existence of a majority population that is still desperately poor and difficult to employ with this idea of what Tunica's boosters would like the county to become. Already, with the rise in land values, those who are ill equipped to take advantage of Tunica's new opportunities are seeing their rents skyrocket while their housing remains substandard. As Clifford Cox, the director of Tunica Habitat for Humanity, observed over coffee in the summer of 1995, "This county is so dollar-signs-in-the-eyes that they're not looking at the small community—the citizens that are already here. They're concentrating on how to bring people in."

Tunica's transformation seems to be off to a good start. One of the county's largest landowners has joined with developers from Memphis to build a planned community in Robinsonville, near the casinos. But some of Tunica's blacks worry that the closer the county's leaders come to realizing their vision, the more marginalized the black population will become. Although an influx of families with good incomes would seem to be a boon to the county's educational system, for instance, Willie Dismuke, the high school principal, assumes that such growth will ultimately result in two public schools, one for affluent white newcomers, one for poor black Tunica natives. (Indeed, a new elementary school to serve the anticipated population boom in the Robinsonville area is now under consideration.) Whether or not events prove Dismuke right, his assumption that Tunica will steadfastly remain two communities even if the county's economy and population change radically shows a striking lack of confidence in Tunica's ability or willingness to allow race relations to change. . . .

Few Rewards for Black Casino Workers

Perhaps most frustrating for the black population is that Tunica does not seem eager to make a place for even those blacks who have been able to take advantage of the new opportunities the casinos have presented to improve their lives. Some black Tunicans have managed to earn enough money working in the casinos to get themselves off welfare. Now they would like to buy houses in the community where their families have lived for generations. Whereas it would seem that these are just the sort of citizens that Tunica might like to keep, the county is in fact offering them little reward for their efforts. Few low-cost, decent houses are available in Tunica, and there seems to be some effort to keep things that way. Perceiving a new market, Bob Hall, a local developer, is trying to build houses that those blacks who are now steadily employed can afford with a Federal Housing Administration loan, and he blames the town's planning commission for trying to stall him. According to Hall, who is white, people argue that they don't want "that kind of housing," which he translates to mean that they don't want "any more houses for black people to live in."

Although Sister Gus Griffin concedes that the white community has become more willing than it was in the past to permit changes that will help the black population, she nevertheless believes that whites on the whole are unlikely "to do anything to make it easier for African-Americans to live in Tunica." Surprisingly, however, given this atmosphere, even those blacks who now have the means to leave Tunica want to stay. A love for the place is one of the few things blacks and whites share in Tunica. Reflecting the views of many in the black community, Freddie Brandon, a board member of a Tunica housing-assistance organization, asserted during a conversation in the fall of 1995, "This is our home; we're not going anywhere."

A White Exurb?

It remains to be seen whether Tunica's gamble on casinos will pay off in the long run. County officials and the Chamber of Commerce eye neighboring states and counties nervously, fearing that if Memphis, for instance, decides to throw its doors open to casinos, a substantial number of Tunica's gamblers will drift away. . . .

Whatever their future, the casinos are booming in Tunica now, and although, located seven miles from the county seat, they have not yet penetrated Tunica's core, they are certainly edging the county into modern America. Dinner out in Tunica used to mean fried catfish or chitterlings at the Blue and White, which caters mostly to whites, or Vada's Diner, which caters mostly to blacks. Now a Tunican need only drive to the Circus Circus casino to order cioppino and tiramisu. More important, the casinos are happy to take everybody's money. "We love to go out to eat out there," Sister Gus says, "to see people of both races sitting down in the same room." As employers, too, the casinos are potentially a progressive force that could push Tunica out of its well-worn groove. They are a source of wealth and opportunity beyond the control of the traditional economic and political powers in the county. And with no interest in anything but turning a profit, they have no stake in maintaining Tunica's caste system.

If the casinos succeed in jarring the county out of decades of economic and social stagnation, Tunica will have an opportunity far more profound than anyone could have imagined just a few years ago: it will have the means to remake itself. If it so chooses, Tunica can use its new resources to prepare its people to take advantage of the chance afforded by the casinos. The county can define its needs as the needs of the majority of its citizens. But if it is true, as one long-time white Tunica resident asserts, echoing an oft-repeated observation, that whites "want things to stay the same; they don't want blacks to get ahead," it is unlikely, to say the least, that Tunica will make this choice. Even if there are many exceptions to this dismal assessment, focusing on changing the lives of the county's poor would mean sacrificing the strides the county could make were it not hampered by this population—sacrificing, in other words, the vision of Tunica as a prosperous white exurb.

To arrive at a thriving exurb of golf courses and retirement condos, those who would re-create the county must essentially see Tunica as a blank canvas. Then they can decide how best to work with the medium they have been given—the casinos—to bring the place (although not necessarily its population) to its fullest potential. Ironically, the economic tide that should be bringing black Tunicans into the mainstream may instead allow white Tunica to push them even further into the backwater, while white Tunicans chase their dream of a prosperous rural southern town—essentially what the town of Tunica would be today if the black areas at its edges could be ignored.

As prosperous people move into Tunica, for instance, they will dilute the force of poverty there by making what is now a poor black majority—with potential, if not actual, political power—an underclass minority. This population will decrease not only in relative size but also in absolute number, as those who cannot take advantage of the new economic opportunities are displaced by the rising rents that accompany prosperity. So although the casinos help to alleviate the county's poverty, they are also a means by which the middle class can distance itself from the poor in Tunica, as it has in much of the rest of the United States. . . .

A Misguided Attitude

Because the county has maintained such a distance between the races, white Tunica can disassociate itself from the county's problems by equating them with the black population—much the way whites in Los Angeles, say, view their city's impoverished minorities as a foreign presence imposed on the place, depressing its economy and culture. Such an attitude, ungenerous everywhere, is especially misguided in Tunica, where blacks have been a majority since the Delta was settled. In fact, if either group can claim more credit for making the Delta prosper, it is the African-Americans. If they belong anywhere, they belong in a place that they built, sharing in its prosperity.

Those who believe and can behave as if the fates of blacks and whites in Tunica are not bound together are fooling themselves. In explaining how the white southerner is defined by the African-American, despite the separation of the races, William Styron has written, "In the South [the African-American] is a perpetual and immutable part of history itself, a piece of the vast fabric so integral and necessary that without him the fabric dissolves." Much as they might wish and work to do so, it is more than a century too late for whites and blacks in the Delta, "the most southern place on earth," to divorce themselves from one another without losing an integral part of themselves.

Games of Chance Promote Valuable Causes Worldwide

Richard McGowan

To raise money for various social causes, many governments around the world sponsor casinos, bingo halls, lotteries, and other betting venues, writes Richard McGowan. In the following selection, he reveals how countries such as Spain, Russia, China, Ireland, Great Britain, and Albania have used games of chance to fund charities, national athletic teams, medical research projects, and schools. McGowan is an economics professor at Boston College in Chestnut Hill, Massachusetts.

Legalized state-sponsored gambling is not a uniquely American phenomenon. Throughout the world, governments sponsor not only lotteries but other forms of gambling as well, including bingo games, casinos, and trackside betting at dog and horse races.

In fact, the number of countries that do not operate lotteries is small. For example, every nation in Europe has a lottery in place. Lotteries among Asian nations, including China, Japan, and Singapore, are common. And even among the impoverished nations of Africa, such as South Africa, Nigeria, and Egypt, people who barely have enough to eat pursue games of chance every day.

All told, revenues spent on lotteries and other state-sponsored gambling enterprises are high: In 1992, the global lottery industry alone accounted for about $80 billion [U.S.] in consumer spending.

Raising Money for Causes

For many countries, lotteries represent efforts on the part of local, state, or central governments to generate money without raising taxes. Meanwhile, other countries—or organizations operating within these countries—use lotteries to raise money for such specific causes as disaster relief, sponsorship of national sports teams, and social welfare. A few examples follow:

• *Spain.* Spaniards have long been avid gamblers, having had access to lotteries since King Carlos III introduced the Spanish lottery in 1763. Government-sanctioned lotteries, in fact, financed the Napoleonic War in 1811 as well as other government enterprises, including large-scale

Reprinted from Richard McGowan, "Games of Chance Promote Valuable Causes Worldwide," *Forum for Applied Research and Public Policy*, Summer 1996, by permission of the publisher.

road and railroad construction in the 18th and 19th centuries. In the twentieth century, Spanish lotteries have funded efforts to clean up rivers and toxic-waste sites.

Today, Spain is second only to the United States in terms of total gambling expenditures. In 1987, Spain spent approximately $22 billion [U.S.] (2.7 trillion Spanish pesetas) on lotteries, slot machines, bingo games, casinos, and horse-race and football pools.

Though Spain no longer turns to lotteries to fund wars, organizations within the country have instituted lotteries to raise funds for worthy causes. For instance, Spain's *Organizacion Nacional de Ciegos* [ONCE] (National Organization for the Blind), a group with approximately 34,000 members, holds a weekly numbers lottery. Lottery patrons can purchase tickets on any street corner from any of 20,000 ticket vendors, many of whom are blind.

In 1992, ticket sales for the lottery amounted to $2.8 billion [U.S.], up from $400,000 [U.S.] in 1989. Half of these revenues are distributed as prize money. Some 3 percent is given to a foundation for the handicapped. The remaining 47 percent is set aside for the organization's 30,000 salaried employees, 20,000 ticket vendors (who are paid three times the minimum wage), and the organization's 15,000 retired employees who earn pensions.

Besides operating a lottery, ONCE boasts investments in construction companies, media organizations, and banks. In fact, ONCE is the fourth or fifth largest investment organization in Spain and is the nation's second largest advertiser.

Thanks in part to its sizeable investment portfolio, ONCE provides a substantial number of jobs, particularly for the blind. In 1989, for example, ONCE created 1,000 jobs; awarded 3,000 scholarships; and constructed hospitals, schools, and recreation centers exclusively for blind people.

Hope and Money

• *Russia.* The Russian people are currently in dire need of two things: hope and money. Over the past few years, lotteries have sought to provide a measure of both. Russia's main lottery, Million Lotto, is intended to raise funds for sports-related activities.

The lottery represents a joint agreement between the financially troubled Russian Olympic Committee and Intracom, a Greek firm that invested $20 million [U.S.] in 1994 to launch a lottery that would support Russian athletes. The Million Lotto's yellow and black kiosks are located throughout Russia and dispense tickets that cost two cents [U.S.] (10 rubles) each.

Average weekly sales for the Million Lotto have been $78,000 [U.S.] (about 35 million rubles), which is modest by U.S. standards; California sells that amount in 10 minutes. The reason: Though 9 million Muscovites are eligible to buy lottery tickets, their average income is only $15 [U.S.] (8,500 rubles) per month. Thus, a Russian could easily spend 20 percent of his or her wages on lottery tickets.

The odds of winning the Russian lottery are slim. In fact, for one of the more popular games the odds are 1 in 14 million, and the largest payout has been $38,000 [U.S.] (22 million rubles). The average prize runs $2,700 [U.S.] (1 million rubles)—more than 200 times the average Muscovite's salary. Unlike the United States, where lottery winners are paraded before television cameras by lottery publicists, in Russia, all winners receive their prizes secretly to prevent theft. . . .

Russia recently introduced a lottery specifically aimed at helping victims of the Chernobyl disaster of 1986. To a large extent, the lottery was the brainchild of Robert Gail, the American bone marrow specialist who traveled to the then Soviet Union to assist in treating the victims of the nuclear disaster.

Gail recognized that, with Russian relief coffers running dry, the victims might well be deprived of life-saving treatments for cancer and radiation poisoning. He established the lottery to generate funds for medical research and care.

The tickets, printed in the United States, went on sale in January 1993 and are sold for $1 [U.S.] (575 rubles), the daily wage for many Russians. Prizes range from $5 to $100,000 [U.S.] (3,000 to 57 million rubles). Since its introduction, the lottery has generated more than $3.5 million [U.S.] (2 trillion rubles) to aid Chernobyl victims.

In 1994, the Russian city of St. Petersburg launched a lottery to support both the 1994 Goodwill Games, which were held at St. Petersburg in 1995, and the Russian teams that competed. Tickets were priced at nine cents [U.S.] (50 rubles), with a top payoff of $3,571 [U.S.] (2 million rubles). The lottery raised more than $1.5 million [U.S.] (84 billion rubles).

Assisting Charities and Sports Teams

• *China.* China introduced the Social Welfare Lottery in July 1987. By September 1992, it had sold more than $780 million [U.S.] (3 billion Yuan) in tickets. More than $270 million [U.S.] (1 billion Yuan) of that money has been placed in the Social Welfare Fund.

Over the years, lottery proceeds have helped find homes for orphans and assist disabled persons who cannot find jobs. Overall, some 17,000 projects of varying scope have been subsidized through lottery revenues. For example, $54 million [U.S.] (200 Yuan) was provided to assist victims of the 1991 flood that swept through northern China.

The lottery employs approximately 2,000 full-time administrators, in addition to the 20,000 who are engaged in printing, storing, transporting, and selling the tickets.

China also has set up several smaller lotteries to benefit its national athletes. For example, a lottery was developed in Shanghai to help finance the inaugural East Asian Games, which were held in Shanghai in 1995. The lottery, in fact, provided more than 40 percent of the funds needed for the games.

• *Ireland.* Ireland's lottery system was established in 1986 and has paid out more than $250 million [U.S.] (160 million Irish pounds) of its $722 million [U.S.] (455 million Irish pounds) revenues to a variety of nonprofit organizations, including those that benefit sports teams, cultural activities, youth groups, and health and social-welfare organizations. For instance, medical research and hospital construction are supported through lottery proceeds. Approximately half the revenues have been awarded as prizes; the typical payout is about $2 million [U.S.] (1.3 million Irish pounds).

There are two lottery games available in Ireland, and nearly 60 percent of adults play them regularly. Tickets are sold through agents who receive 6.3 percent of revenue; another 10 percent is held for administrative costs.

For all the good they've done, Ireland's lotteries have posed one unwelcome side-effect. While lotteries have raised considerable funds for worthy causes, they have contributed to a sense of complacency among Irish citizens, many of whom believe that their favorite charities no longer need direct donations.

For instance, though nearly 90 percent of Ireland's 3.5 million people donate to charities at least once a month, 25 percent of the more popular charitable organizations claim that their charitable income has declined since Ireland introduced its national lottery.

National Lotteries

• *Great Britain.* In 1994, Great Britain became the last European country to develop a lottery. Due to the popularity of lotteries throughout Europe and America, many people and a host of public officials in Britain have been calling for games of their own for many years. Lottery officials are hoping for annual revenues of $2 billion [U.S.] (1.3 billion British pounds). This represents per capita spending of $18 per year [U.S.] (11.5 British pounds).

Like Ireland, players will have two games from which to choose: a lotto game played through computerized terminals in shops all over Britain and an instant "scratch and win" game.

Tickets will cost about one pound for the lotto game. Officials expect jackpots to reach $1.5 million [U.S.] (960,000 British pounds), although many smaller prizes also will be awarded. About 30 percent of the revenues will be awarded to charities devoted to the arts, culture, and sports.

About 70 percent of British adults already gamble, spending on average about $7 [U.S.] (4.5 British pounds) per capita each week. Most people—about 16 million in all—place their money in soccer pools, which currently net more than $500 million [U.S.] (320 million British pounds) for the British treasury each year. Pool operators fear that a national lottery may reduce their operations by as much as 30 percent, forcing them to cut their work force from 6,500 to 3,000.

• *Albania.* Before the 1992 Summer Olympic Games in Barcelona, Albania was hoping to make its first Olympic appearance since 1972. The country found itself in need of funding, so it turned to a lottery for help.

Tickets in the national lottery cost about 50 cents [U.S.] (50 leks), and prizes range up to $5,000 [U.S.] (500,000 leks), which is twice the average annual salary in Albania.

Revenues generated by the lottery enabled Albania to send a team to the 1992 Olympics. The government decided to continue the initiative, and since 1992 sufficient revenues were generated to build a training center and to ensure Albanian athletes were represented in the 1996 Olympics in Atlanta.

A Sure Thing

When it comes to lotteries, the bottom line is this: Games of chance are accepted throughout the world as an effective way to collect public monies for worthwhile causes that would otherwise go underfunded.

LOTTERY ADS DECEIVE THE PUBLIC

Joshua Wolf Shenk

Lottery ads often induce gambling by implying that constant betting will make players rich, argues Joshua Wolf Shenk in the following selection. However, he points out, these ads are deceitful because they conceal the slim chances of winning and overstate the size of the jackpots. Moreover, since lotteries are not restricted by government truth-in-advertising standards, lottery ads can create fictitious stories about winnings, he contends. Such techniques are reprehensible because they lure the poor and the addicted into gambling, Shenk maintains. Shenk is an editor of the *Washington Monthly*, a journal of liberal political opinion.

Tom had been playing the lottery for two years when God started whispering in his ear. At first, Tom (who asked that his last name be withheld) would spend just a few dollars a week. He had his regular numbers, and he'd play them when he thought of it.

But then, he says, on the days that he hadn't planned on playing, the word would come from Heaven: Your number is coming *tonight*. Fear would strike him like ice water on the neck: "I'd think, 'I'm not going to win it. I don't have the [money] on that number.'" So he'd rush out to play his regular number, and many more. Before long, he was spending $300 a week on tickets.

"It was 'A Dollar and a Dream'; 'Hey, You Never Know,'" he says, repeating the advertising slogans of the New York lottery. Tom pauses. "Those were good come-ons."

Lottery Ads Are Effective

It's no accident that the voices inside Tom's head echoed lottery ads. They're extremely effective. And they're everywhere: on the radio and TV, in bus shelters and on billboards, even in mailings sent straight to homes. The message is simple: Play the lottery and get rich. Get rich, and all your problems will be solved. The New York lottery takes in more than $2 billion in sales each year, and it spends $30 million each year on advertising to keep the cash rolling in.

State lotteries target anyone who might cough up a dollar (or $10 or $20) for the chance to strike it rich. Conveniently silent on the odds, these ads send the message that hard work and patience is for suckers. In the process, the ads help wring billions of dollars from the most vulnerable "customers" possible—the poor and the addicted.

Criticism of state lotteries runs a wide gamut. Some say the state shouldn't even *allow* gambling, much less conduct it. Others argue that gambling should be left in private hands. Still others believe that the state should run lotteries for roughly the same reason many states run liquor stores: to keep the business controlled and clean, and to make money for the state.

Regardless of where you stand on these important questions, though, one thing should be clear: The advertising that entices Americans to spend tens of billions of dollars on lottery tickets each year is deceitful and corrosive. It is the only form of advertising unburdened by state and federal truth-in-advertising standards. The fact that it comes from the state—which ought to encourage people's strengths, not prey on their weaknesses—makes it all the more foul.

As of 1995, 37 states and the District of Columbia had instituted lotteries, and that number is likely to grow. "Quite simply, states need the revenue," explains David Gale, executive director of the North American Association of State and Provincial Lotteries. "Every dollar raised by the lottery is a dollar you don't need to get from taxes." Across the country, $34 billion in lottery tickets were sold in 1994. In Texas, the lottery contributed $935 million to the state's budget. In New York, the figure was $1.01 billion. As states have become dependent on lottery revenue, the pressure to keep people playing has become relentless. "Marketing is absolutely essential," Gale says. "Lottery tickets are no different than any other product. Your market will lose interest after a while. You have to keep after them."

Like any sophisticated business, lotteries target the specific groups of people most susceptible to suggestion. The Iowa lottery's media plan, for example, contains the following statement of objective: "To target our message demographically against those that we know to be heavy users."

Targeting the Poor

One such target is the poor. The charge that lotteries are regressive— that is, hitting lower-income residents the hardest—makes intuitive sense, since the pitch of wealthy fantasies clearly resonates most strongly among those who are least affluent. "There's absolutely no question about it," says Charles Clotfelter, a Duke University economist and a leading authority on lotteries. According to a study by the Heartland Institute, a conservative think tank, the poor spend more money than the non-poor on lotteries—not only as a percentage of their income, but also in absolute terms. Blacks and Hispanics also tend to play more often than whites.

I worked two summers at an Ohio convenience store that sold lottery tickets, and my experience there confirms these findings. The store drew customers from all socioeconomic backgrounds, but lottery players fell into distinct categories. On a normal day, the lottery patrons were mostly working-class blacks. When the jackpots for Super Lotto got sky-high, some wealthier folks joined the lines. But the staple customers—those who spent five, 20, or 40 dollars a day on daily numbers and scratch-off games—were the same people every day: not executives or store managers playing for kicks, but postal workers and retirees on Social Security. You'll see the same trend at almost any lottery outlet. You'll also notice that the same stores almost invariably sell liquor and cigarettes. Choose your poison.

The image of miserable working people magically transported to lives of wealth and ease is a staple of lottery ads. A billboard once placed in a slum of Chicago read simply: "Your Ticket Out of Here." An ad for the D.C. lottery shows a man "before" the lottery—with matted hair, stubble on his face, and glasses—and "after"—freshly washed and clean-shaven, wearing a tuxedo, and holding the program for a theater performance. The copy reads: "Just One Ticket . . . And It Could Happen to You." An ad for the Michigan lottery shows a college kid piloting a Lear jet. Then it cuts to him day-dreaming on the job at a fast food restaurant. "Thirty new Lotto millionaires were created last year," the announcer states. "Play the Lotto, and you could win the stuff dreams are made of."

Targeting Compulsive Gamblers

Lottery ads also go after gambling addicts, using a message tuned to their weaknesses. About 5 percent of the population is susceptible to compulsive gambling, according to Dr. Valerie Lorenz, executive director of the Compulsive Gambling Center in Baltimore. In many cases, she says, lottery ads help tip these people over the edge.

Remember Tom's greatest fear, that his number would fall on a day he hadn't bet? This is one of the defining characteristics of compulsive gamblers, and it's a button that lotteries push incessantly. "Don't forget to play every day," the Pennsylvania lottery ad says. Many ads picture disheartened would-be winners whose numbers came up on a day they declined or forgot to play. One ad for Tri-State Megabucks (in New Hampshire, Maine, and Vermont), for example, shows a pathetic man grilling hamburgers on a fire escape, while scenes of wealth and grandeur flash by. The theme is set to the tune of "It Had to Be You."

> It could have been you.
> It could have been you.
> Countin' the dough,
> Ready to go, on that three-month cruise.
> Walkin' in style, down easy street,
> Wearin' a smile, it could have been sweet.
> But what can I say?

You just didn't play.
It could have been youuuuu!

The theme of magical, instant transformation also lures problem gamblers. "They live in a very painful world," says Dr. Lorenz. "They want to escape into fantasy, and they want it instantly." And, of course, the sheer regularity of the ads is a curse to addicts trying to stay on the straight-and-narrow. "I hear this all the time from lottery addicts who are in recovery," Lorenz says. "They'll cover their ears or their heads. They'll say, 'I wish I could leave the state.' But that wouldn't help. It's all over the country."

The ads never mention the losers. Tom Cummings, executive director of the Massachusetts Council on Compulsive Gambling, told me about two women he has been counseling. "One lost her house after going $40,000 in debt playing the lottery," he said. "The other gambled away money that was supposed to pay for her daughter's education. All on the lottery."

Systematic Distortion

Lotteries aren't alone in suggesting that their product has magical qualities—that's the art of advertising. But lottery ads take a prize when it comes to their systematic distortion. Because the lotteries are chartered by state legislatures, they're untouchable by federal regulators and they consider state regulators their colleagues in public service. This allows lotteries to conceal the astronomical odds against winning and inflate the size of jackpots.

Consider a 1993 California radio spot profiling a lottery winner: "John Padgett went to bed on Saturday night a regular guy," the announcer says. "When he woke up, he was worth $11 million. That's because he's Super Lotto winner number 610."

Well, not quite. Padgett did win an $11.5 million jackpot. But that's not *worth* $11.5 million. Any prize over a million dollars is paid out over 20 years. Padgett's annual payment came to $575,000. After taxes, the actual yearly award is worth around $400,000. And the lost value—due to both inflation ($400,000 will be worth far less in 2013 than it is today) and lost interest—is significant.

It may be hard to sympathize with someone receiving a $400,000 check every year. But this ad—and nearly every state uses a similar pitch—is clearly misleading. The government would never allow similar distortions from private sector advertisers.

Finance companies, for example, are explicitly forbidden to air commercials that feature investors who have earned vast sums of money with the message, "It could be you." But lotteries do just that. "I was probably going to have to go back to work to make ends meet," Kentucky lottery winner Denise Golden says in one ad. "And now I won't have to. . . . It's a dream come true."

Unfair Tactics

Lotteries are also exempt from Federal Trade Commission truth-in-advertising standards and rules that, to give just one example, require contests and sweepstakes to clearly state the odds against winning in every advertisement. Omitting the odds is a crucial element of lotteries' media strategy, since they're trying to convince people that if they play long enough, they are certain to hit the jackpot. "Sooner than later," says an ad for the West Virginia lottery, "you're gonna win!" "We won't stop until everyone's a millionaire," the New York lottery promises.

A clue as to how far lotteries exceed the bounds that constrain other advertisers is indicated by a report from the National Association of Broadcasters (NAB) issued in 1975. Three tactics seemed clearly out of bounds, the NAB concluded:

1. [Indicating] what fictitious winners may do, hope to do or have done with their winnings.

2. [Using] unqualified or inaccurate language regarding potential winners' winnings. (e.g. "There's a pot of gold for those who buy lottery tickets"; "Buy a ticket and be a winner.")

3. [Utilizing] approaches which praise people who buy lottery tickets or denigrate people who do not buy tickets.

Today's lotteries hold themselves to no such standards. The only rule is to produce maximum profit. Even in Virginia and Texas, two states that forbid their lotteries to "induce" people to play, ads make gambling seem fun and glamorous. Missouri originally required all its lottery ads to include a disclaimer: "This message . . . is not intended to induce any person to participate in the lottery or purchase a lottery ticket." The disclaimer was dropped in 1988. It was thought to be hurting sales.

Accounting Tricks

Lotteries defend themselves against criticism by citing the revenue they raise. They also advertise to publicize their role in funding state projects. (Not only does this approach bolster political support, it's also a shrewd ploy to hook more players. Gambling is fun—and it's also a public service!)

Each state has its own slogan: "When Colorado plays, everybody wins." "The Missouri lottery: It makes life a little richer for all of us." The premise of these ads—and a crucial element of lotteries' popularity—is that money goes to improving favorite areas of state spending, like schools or parks. But this is a mere accounting trick. Ohio claims that its lottery revenue goes toward education, for example. "But that doesn't mean that the budget for education grows by that much,"

David Gale explains. "What happens is, the legislature budgets this much for education. They see the lottery will contribute this much. So they take the money they would have spent on education and put it to other uses."

Most states avoid the fiction altogether and say outright that the money goes to the general fund. But that doesn't stop lotteries from claiming credit for the very best of state government. On its 20th anniversary, the Maryland lottery ran a series of "public service" ads. One pictured a nurse holding an infant, saying the baby would get better care because of the Maryland lottery. Another ad in the series gave credit to the lottery for the high school graduation of an inner-city black teenager.

It is true that lottery profits go to state treasuries. But so do taxes. Taxes are also honestly raised and reflect community decisions about how to fairly distribute burdens and responsibilities. In the current political climate, raising lottery revenue is a political virtue; raising taxes is political death. Naturally, politicians choose the easy route. New York Governor George Pataki recently announced plans for an enormous tax cut. He intends to make up the loss in revenue through the introduction of "five minute keno" in liquor stores and bars, which is expected to net the state $115 million per year.

Promoting Gambling Is Inexcusable

Lotteries defend themselves by pointing out the obvious: No one is forced to buy a lottery ticket. "I get so angry when people say they should decide how [others] should spend their money," says Teresa La Fleur, who publishes books and a magazine for the lottery industry. "Unless we decide it's wrong to gamble, it's just a fact of life that people are going to make choices with their money."

But states don't merely allow, or provide, gambling. They stimulate it. In addition to running ads, some states even conduct direct-mail campaigns, sending coupons for free tickets via mail. In a typical campaign, cited in *Selling Hope: State Lotteries in America*, by Clotfelter and co-author Phillip Cook, 35 to 40 percent of the coupons were redeemed for lottery tickets. One-third of those who redeemed the coupons were new players; one-third of these new players began to play regularly.

Considering the addictiveness of lotteries, these types of promotions are inexcusable. Of the nearly 40,000 calls to the Council on Compulsive Gambling in New Jersey in 1994, for example, 52 percent complained of addiction to lottery games. Imagine the outcry if Philip Morris sent free packs of cigarettes through the mail.

In fact, the parallel between cigarettes and lottery tickets is uncanny. That's why both have been the subject of strict limits on advertising. Until 1974, when Congress repealed a ban on the promotion of gambling in the mass media, TV stations couldn't so much as mention winning numbers. Now, of course, TV is the most popular medium of advertising. Besides the many commercials, lottery drawings are televised and a number of states have half-hour game shows centered around the lottery.

Congressman Jim McCrery, a Republican from Louisiana, has introduced legislation requiring the Federal Trade Commission to impose truth-in-advertising standards on lotteries. That would be a start. But a more dramatic step—banning ads altogether—is in order. [McCrery's legislation did not pass.]

Lottery ads don't just sell a product. They sell a way of life. One ad for the Washington state lottery shows a line of workers punching their time clock. "The true joys in life," the announcer says, "are not found in the empty pursuit of pleasure, but in the accomplishments realized through one's own hard labor. For nothing satisfies the soul so much as honest toil, and seeing through a job well done." Then the man at the end of the line takes his timesheet and throws it out the window. "Of course, having a whole bunch of money's not bad either."

When will public officials stop for a moment, and listen to what they're saying—that hard work and patience are for suckers, that civic virtue is a function of how much you spend on the lottery? "Even in these cynical times," says Clotfelter, "government has some moral capital. So when the government says 'Children, stay in school'; 'Husbands, don't beat your wives'—these have some value to them. If you take that capital and use it [the way lotteries do], one has to ask, does this serve the intention of the state?"

THE HIDDEN ADDICTION:
COMPULSIVE GAMBLING

Arnie Wexler and Sheila Wexler

Arnie Wexler, a recovering gambling addict, is a certified compulsive gambling counselor and the founder of New Jersey's Council on Compulsive Gambling. His wife, Sheila Wexler, is a certified alcohol and drug counselor and a certified compulsive gambling counselor who developed a compulsive gambling treatment program at New Hope Foundation in Marlboro, New Jersey. In the following selection, the Wexlers define compulsive gambling as a progressive disease akin to alcoholism and drug addiction. They maintain that compulsive gambling is especially insidious because it can be easily concealed until the gambler's life has nearly been destroyed by the addiction. Pathological gamblers need counseling to recover from their addiction, the authors assert.

Tom called the gamblers' hotline from a telephone booth on the boardwalk in Atlantic City, New Jersey. The 22-year-old's options were exhausted and he talked about suicide. He was $75,000 in debt, had no job, and had recently lost $4,000 in stolen money. The hotline volunteer helped him enroll in a freestanding, inpatient facility for gamblers. During admission, Tom revealed that he had been in several treatment centers for drug addiction, but was never questioned about his gambling problem.

• Steve came to treatment after a gambling binge in the casinos of Atlantic City. He was experiencing what appeared to be withdrawal symptoms. His pupils were dilated, he was sweating and shaking, and he suffered extreme mood swings. The nursing staff reported that his blood pressure was elevated and that he was extremely agitated. His denial of alcohol or drug use was later confirmed through lab tests. Steve was placed in a detoxification unit until he was stabilized.

• Michelle had been clean and sober for 14 months. She never revealed to her addictions counselor that gambling was her first true love. During the 14 months in recovery, her attendance at the racetrack went from occasional to daily. One day, she found herself at the

Reprinted from Arnie Wexler and Sheila Wexler, "The Hidden Addiction," *Professional Counselor*, June 1997, by permission of the authors.

track's bar preparing to order a drink. Instead, she picked up the phone and called Gamblers Anonymous. Today she has 11 years of abstinence from gambling and 12 years from drugs and alcohol.

Gambling Addiction

As these case studies reveal, gambling addiction presents many of the same symptoms and manifestations as addiction to alcohol and drugs. Yet the disease can be much more insidious because it is more difficult to detect and can have a more devastating effect on friends and families. It is also growing rapidly and reaching victims not yet in their teens. Over the past several years, we have conducted workshops and seminars on the subject of compulsive gambling for counselors from Canada to Mississippi, from Vermont to California, and even as far away as Japan. The one thing all these counselors have in common is that they all report a daily increase in the number of calls for help they are receiving from gamblers and their families.

Whether it involves scratching a lottery ticket, a weekly poker game with neighbors, a small game of bingo in a church basement, or a high-stakes game of baccarat at a Las Vegas casino, gambling feeds a basic need for excitement. It is wagering something of value on an unpredictable event for the opportunity of winning more than was wagered. For many, gambling can remain a social activity, a harmless and entertaining diversion from everyday life. However, what seems like a moment of elation or exhilaration for some, can for others become an overriding compulsion. These people cannot resist the impulse to gamble, and become pathological. Social, non-pathological gamblers differ from compulsive gamblers in that they can quit gambling at any time, win or lose. This is due to three factors: 1) there is no self-esteem tied to winning or losing; 2) other aspects of their lives are more important and rewarding; 3) they rarely have a big win.

With compulsive gamblers, the opposite is true. They fail to resist impulses to gamble, and their gambling behavior compromises their personal lives. They may give up any and all activities not connected to gambling. Honeymoons and family vacations are planned where gambling is available. Alienation from friends and family occurs, because the compulsive gambler becomes easily bored in social situations and prefers to socialize with others who have a similar lifestyle.

A Progressive Disease

Compulsive gambling is a progressive disease. Its sufferers have an uncontrollable preoccupation and urge to gamble excessively, leading to the compromise, disruption and destruction of the gambler's personal life, family relationships, finances, and career or vocation. The disease progresses rapidly, advancing from the need for a little excitement or a quick profit, to an all-consuming preoccupation that becomes for the addict a matter of life and death. Like alcoholics who will drain the bottom of a bottle of vanilla extract for the alcohol, like drug addicts who will steal from their own families to support their habits, gamblers will do whatever they need to do to secure one more fix—a bet. They will continue until nothing is left: employment, savings, family assets, anything that may be borrowed, sold, pawned, or stolen.

For compulsive gamblers, the simple act of placing a bet is similar both emotionally and physiologically to taking a drink or a hit of a drug. Many gamblers who were also addicted to alcohol or drugs have reported getting the same rush and euphoria from gambling as from chemicals. It represents a loss of control and the beginning of an inescapable compulsion.

However, there is a fundamental difference. Gamblers don't reveal the signs of their addictions through alcoholic breath or erratic behavior. There is no slurred speech, no track marks on the arms. A urinalysis test won't reveal the problem. Because there is little, if any, outward indication of a problem during these early stages, gamblers find it much easier to conceal their addiction, making intervention more difficult and allowing the disease to more easily and rapidly progress into the advanced stages.

The Phases of Compulsive Gambling

Compulsive gamblers pass through three phases. The first is the winning phase, during which they report a series of wins or streaks. This phase usually takes place over a short period of time; however, winning can occur during all phases. Most compulsive gamblers report at least one "big win," the hook that encourages the fantasy that they will continue to win and become wealthy from their gambling activities.

The next phase is the losing phase, during which gamblers begin to chase their losses. As bets get larger, they begin borrowing money from family, friends, co-workers, credit card accounts, banks, and eventually illegal sources in order to cover their wagers. They often delay paying debts and will manipulate finances in order to obtain money for gambling. They will lie to cover up their habits and are often irritable, restless, and argumentative. They may attempt to slow down or quit gambling altogether, but will find themselves unable to stay away for any length of time.

The last phase of progression is appropriately referred to as the desperation phase. Gamblers spend most of their waking hours in pursuit of the bet and/or the money to make the bet. By now the thrill ends when the bet is placed, not after the win or the loss. The outcome is irrelevant. The excitement of a win is diminished because the winnings will only be bet again immediately. At this point, gamblers have alienated themselves from family and friends. They may begin involvement in illegal acts, i.e., bad checks, theft, embezzlement, or credit card fraud. They experience feelings of hopelessness and despair. Suicidal thoughts and attempts are not uncommon. Their partners will also experience feelings of hopelessness and may consider suicide.

Now the gambling is so out of control that gamblers may destroy not only their own lives but those of their family members and/or significant others. They argue frequently and feel deeper rejection, fear, anger, worry, and anxiety as the spiral of progression continues. They tend to blame themselves and make vain attempts to gain control of the money and the gambling. Financial problems and pressures are overwhelming, and they find themselves unable to cope with everyday life. Yet they may appear to function capably on the job or elsewhere because of the hidden nature of the addiction.

As was the case with alcoholism for many years, compulsive gambling is, for the most part, unrecognized and often misunderstood. Perhaps this is due to the fact that compulsive gambling is a "drugless" addiction. Gamblers get high without substances, yet they experience the same reactions and symptoms as do the abusers of chemicals: preoccupation, denial, tolerance, loss of control, and withdrawal. Gambling can elicit stimulating, tranquilizing, and/or pain-relieving responses. It is used as a way to escape or relieve a dysphoric mood.

Profiles in Gambling

The average compulsive gambler has an IQ above 120. Ninety-six percent started gambling before age 14. Abundant energy and unreasonable optimism are common traits. They are characteristically risk-takers, especially in financial ventures. They become restless and irritable when not gambling, and will try to avoid conflict by lying, distorting, or exaggerating. Gamblers often become hypercritical and may blame others for gambling losses. They will brag about winnings, minimize losses, increase the amounts wagered, and become remorseful over losing.

Though most compulsive gamblers are men, nearly one-third are women, and the percentage is growing. As the baby boom generation ages, the average age of the compulsive gambler also rises. But perhaps the most alarming demographic is among children. By mid-adolescence, hundreds of thousands of teenagers are already compulsive gamblers. A recent survey of 50 New Jersey high schools showed that more than 90 percent of the students had gambled at least once during the year and more than 30 percent gamble at least once a week. Bookmakers and betting rings are found on virtually all college campuses and at many high schools as well. Casinos routinely turn away hundreds of thousands of underage gamblers.

Compulsive gamblers are characterized as successful and strong-willed. They will do whatever is necessary to continue to survive and convince those around them that they are normal. They usually appear to be exemplary and dedicated employees. They are often the ones who run the office football pool. Their powers of persuasion and deception can be highly developed.

Often, gamblers' cover-ups and manipulations can be so convincing that their spouses begin to question their own judgment. They may blame themselves for the family's financial woes and begin to doubt their own worthiness. They may feel unwanted or unloved, a second choice to their spouses' gambling activities. As the cycle of hopelessness continues, partners find it difficult to cope with even the simplest tasks. Money for food, gas, child care, and other basic needs is usually gambled away before it can be used. Children may feel neglected, and possibly suffer emotional and physical abuse.

The partners of gamblers many times experience a negative progression of their own, withdrawing from the company of others, ashamed to admit their loved ones' gambling problems. They may sit at home alone day after day, afraid of being deserted by their gambling spouses. At the depths of despair, they may suffer from nervous breakdowns, may begin using alcohol and drugs to cope, and/or may consider divorce or suicide as the only available options.

Estimates put the number of compulsive gamblers in this country at between 10 million and 12 million, approximately 5 percent of the general population. However, the numbers are much higher among alcoholics and drug addicts. In a survey of New Jersey treatment centers in the late '80s, 28 percent of patients receiving inpatient treatment, and 22 percent receiving outpatient treatment for chemical dependency had gambling as a co-addiction. In some cases, gambling was the primary addiction. The potential for cross-addiction or switching addictions is quite high in this population. Unfortunately, many cases slip through the cracks.

Like alcoholics and drug addicts, gamblers have "enablers" whose compassion and/or ignorance help the gamblers feed their addiction. Friends and family members try to "rescue" compulsive gamblers with a bailout, mistakenly convinced that the gamblers will end their habits if they can find the money to pay off their gambling debts. Bailouts, however, only enable the gambler to continue the addiction and delay the "bottoming out" process. The answer is to neither shut out nor bail out the gambler. It is to get help through counseling.

THE SPREAD OF CASINOS AND THE RISE IN GAMBLING ADDICTION

Valerie C. Lorenz

The proliferation of casinos in the 1990s has resulted in an increase in compulsive gambling, argues Valerie C. Lorenz in the following selection. She contends, furthermore, that the rise in compulsive gambling has exacted social costs such as broken homes, bankruptcies, poverty, increased substance abuse, and higher crime rates. To curb this trend, she believes the federal government should establish an office to research the consequences of widespread gambling and to examine potential gambling regulations, public education possibilities, and funding for compulsive gambling treatment programs. Lorenz is the executive director of the Compulsive Gambling Center in Baltimore, Maryland. This selection was originally presented as a statement before a 1994 congressional committee examining the impact of casino proliferation.

My name is Valerie Lorenz. I have specialized in the field of compulsive gambling for over twenty years. I am Executive Director of the Compulsive Gambling Center, Inc. (formerly National Center for Pathological Gambling, Inc.), a not-for-profit organization providing treatment, education, training, research, and program implementation in the field of compulsive gambling. The Center also operated the oldest national 24-hour Compulsive Gambling Hotline for seven years (discontinued in July 1994 for lack of funding). I served as Co-Chair of the 2-year Task Force on Gambling Addiction in Maryland, and have been Director of the Forensic Center for Compulsive Gambling, specializing in expert witness in testimony and forensic reports for over ten years. I have been a member of the editorial board of *The Journal of Gambling Studies* since 1985, and I have published extensively on the problems of compulsive gambling. I have testified numerous times in this area before state and federal legislative bodies, including the White House Conference on Families.

I am pleased to appear before this Committee today to answer your questions about the impact of casino proliferation. I applaud

Reprinted from the testimony of Valerie C. Lorenz before the U.S. House of Representatives Committee on Small Business at the hearing titled *The National Impact of Casino Gambling Proliferation*, September 21, 1994.

your asking such questions, and encourage this committee to expand this exploration into all types of legalized gambling. And I encourage this Committee to be the leader in establishing national policy on gambling.

An Increase in Problem Gambling

Let me make something very clear: *All* types of gambling can become addictive, regardless of whether one gambles on or with machines, races, tickets or games. Fortunately, only certain people will become gambling addicts. However, the number of compulsive gamblers has been increasing at an alarming rate in the past twenty years—ever since the spread of casinos and state lotteries, which has turned this country into a nation of gamblers. These gamblers spent $394 billion in 1993 on gambling—money that was not spent in local shopping centers, pizza parlors or corner groceries, monies that in seven years could pay off our national debt.

Until the mid-1970s, the typical compulsive gambler was a white, middle-aged, middle-class male. A dozen years ago, a female compulsive gambler was a rarity. Lottery addicts were just beginning to surface. Teenage compulsive gamblers and senior citizens addicted to gambling were nonexistent.

The profile of today's compulsive gambler is truly democratic, all ages, races, religious persuasions, socio-economic levels and education. Sixteen or sixty, the desperation and devastation is the same.

The New Jersey Casino Control Commission regularly reports 25,000 or more teenagers being stopped at the door or ejected from the floors of Atlantic City casinos. One can only guess at how many teenagers do get in, gamble, and are served drinks. Today, research indicates that as many as 7% of teenagers may be addicted to gambling.

Adult gambling addiction has increased from .77% of the adult population (U.S. Commission on the Review of the National Policy Toward Gambling, 1975) to as much as 11% in some states in 1993. Why? Because our governments are saying, "Gambling is OK" and because gambling is now so readily available, with so very little regulation.

The Costs of Compulsive Gambling

The formula is quite simple: Availability leads to more gamblers which leads to more compulsive gamblers. Casino gambling, now in 21 states, is particularly onerous because of the allure of escaping into fantasy, the fast action, and emphasis on quick money, all of which are basic factors in gambling addiction.

Gambling addiction increases socio-economic costs far greater than any amount of revenue generated for the government by the gambling industry. For instance, in 1990, the Maryland Task Force on Gambling Addiction found that Maryland's 50,000 compulsive gamblers cost the state $1.5 billion per year in lost work productivity and monies that are abused (stolen, embezzled, state taxes not paid, etc.). The total cumulative indebtedness of Maryland's compulsive gamblers is $4 billion. That means a lot of small and large businesses are not getting paid, which means they will have to reduce their work force or close up shop.

Other costs resulting from compulsive gambling are broken homes, physical and mental health problems, increase in social and welfare services, indebtedness, bankruptcies, and crime. Each and every one of these are far-reaching, affecting neighbors, employers, entire communities, and generations to come. These direct and indirect costs are staggering.

Taking just the issue of crime alone, virtually all compulsive gamblers, sooner or later, resort to illegal activities to support their gambling addiction. After all, money is the substance of their addiction, and when legal access to money is no longer available, these addicts will commit crimes. The crimes are typically of a non-violent, financial nature, such as fraud or embezzlement or failure to pay taxes. About 25% of them are charged with criminal violations, and about 15% face incarceration. It costs about $20,000 per year for the U.S. Bureau of Prisons to keep one young, healthy compulsive gambler in jail. This cost can escalate to $50,000 for the ailing senior citizen. Then there are the costs for half-way houses, electronic monitoring, and supervised parole and probation.

While in jail, the gambling addict is neither gainfully employed nor paying federal or state taxes. The family may be surviving on drastically reduced income or be on welfare. Well-paying jobs for felons are hard to come by, which means the gambling addict will most likely be earning less in future years, after he or she is released from prison.

Further, compulsive gamblers tend to have a very high rate of civil violations, such as motor vehicle infractions. Probably as much as 90% of casino addicts resort to reckless driving, speeding, and falling asleep at the wheel, resulting in accidents, either to or from the casino. They are a menace on the highway, worse than drunk drivers. Yet what is being done about that, other than to raise the costs of law enforcement and medical care?

Co-Addictions

About two thirds of compulsive gamblers come from homes with an alcoholic parent. Some compulsive gamblers are alcoholics first, maintain sobriety but turn to another addiction, gambling. Other compulsive gamblers may be co-addicted to either alcohol, drugs, or both. Ironically, while there are many education, prevention and treatment programs for the substance abuser, supported by state and federal monies, what is there for the individual who becomes addicted to a government licensed or sponsored activity, gambling? Pathetically little in a few states, nothing in most.

In 1988, Congress passed the Indian Reservation Gambling Act. Some 80% of incarcerated Native Americans have an alcohol problem. Yet what is being done to prevent gambling cross-addiction or co-addiction among them? And by whom? The casinos historically have failed to take any measure of responsibility for compulsive gambling, and only recently have a few Indian Reservations addressed this potential problem among their own people or among their customers. In short, the greed of the gambling industry is matched only by its lack of concern for its customers or the community in which it operates. That is not good business.

Maryland first recognized compulsive gambling to be a serious socio-economic problem in its state in 1978, and funded the first public treatment program. (The first in the nation was established in 1971 at the Brecksville, Ohio, VA Medical Center.) Today, the state does not allocate a single dollar to combat compulsive gambling. Why not? Because every legislative bill introduced to aid compulsive gamblers was fought by the gambling industry—the state lottery, the charitable casinos, the race track, tavern associations, fraternal clubs with video poker machines, and bingo parlors.

What is the end result of widespread casino gambling? Just look at the housing and poverty in Atlantic City, the lack of quality of life in Deadwood, South Dakota, or the alcoholism and crime rate in Las Vegas.

What Should Be Done

What must this government do to contain this national health problem, one that has been labelled "The Addiction of the Nineties"?

First of all, it must face the fact that the problem exists, instead of continuing to ignore it or minimize it. Secondly, it must stop believing the deceptions perpetrated by the gambling industry, that legalization of casinos or race tracks or lotteries are the answer to governments' fiscal woes, the answer to unemployment, or the way to stop tax increases.

This government needs to establish an office to look at the negative consequences of widespread gambling, and it needs to establish comprehensive policy: how much gambling, where, what hours, who will run the game, why, how much money is needed for law enforcement and crime prevention, what is the uniform minimum age, what research is needed, who will educate the public, business and industry, or train health providers, who will fund prevention and treatment programs?

State legislatures across the country are seeking to implement new forms of gambling. One riverboat quickly becomes thirty riverboats in one area. Yet there are less than a dozen professional inpatient treatment programs for compulsive gamblers. The maximum bed capacity is approximately one hundred.

The number of compulsive gamblers in this country today runs into the millions. Who will provide the treatment, and who will pay for it? Not the gambling addicts—they have neither the money nor the health insurance—that was spent at the casinos or on other gambling.

This country can ill afford to ignore the problems caused by the proliferation of gambling and the resultant increase in compulsive gambling. We do not need the economic ruin, broken homes and crime brought on by this industry, which encourages instant gratification, something for nothing, while making a mockery of family, work and community. This country needs your concern and your action.

AMERICA'S UNWARRANTED HYSTERIA OVER CASINOS

Stephen Chapman

Syndicated columnist Stephen Chapman argues that the spread of casinos throughout the United States has been unfairly denounced. Contrary to the opinions of gambling's critics, he maintains, the spread of casinos has not fostered crime, poverty, pathological gambling, or economic damage to communities. Because most casino patrons are rational and responsible, they should continue to enjoy the right to gamble, Chapman concludes.

"Live and let live" is the quintessential American attitude, but it goes out the window when the subject is gambling. The spread of casinos beyond Las Vegas and Atlantic City has been greeted with intense criticism—usually consisting of vigorous speculation and wild exaggeration mixed with a moralism that makes the New England Puritans sound like the soul of tolerance.

Pat Buchanan says that "gambling should return to the swamp whence it came." [Former] Christian Coalition leader Ralph Reed blames it for "destroying families, stealing food from the mouths of children, turning wives into widows." Plenty of liberals echo these pitiful lamentations. *New York Times* columnist Frank Rich says that places with casinos are afflicted by corruption, failing retailers, crime, alcoholism and deepening poverty—making them "a nightmare vision."

Is Wagering Wicked?

To critics, casinos look like Satan's playground. But to some people, anything fun looks suspicious. The view of wagering as wicked is hard to square with the personal experiences of millions of Americans who have visited casinos and found them highly overrated as dens of iniquity.

Why is there such hysteria at the sight of competent adults spending a little of their time and money on a harmless diversion? Casinos alarm conservatives, who worry about letting people think they can get something for nothing, while infuriating liberals, who resent the

Reprinted from Stephen Chapman, "The Unwarranted Hysteria over Casinos," *Conservative Chronicle*, July 3, 1996, by permission of Stephen Chapman and Creators Syndicate.

idea of corporations making money off the gullible. Gambling triggers the conservative impulse to police personal morality as well as the liberal urge to suppress the functioning of soulless economic markets.

Much of the opposition, of course, stems from a fear of the side effects that supposedly come with slot machines and roulette tables. Opponents delight in portraying casino gambling as a fountain of social wreckage. But most of the debris is imaginary.

Contrary to myth, casinos don't pull lawlessness in their wake. Jeremy Margolis, who was superintendent of the Illinois State Police when 13 riverboat casinos began operating there, testified to Congress in 1995 that in the communities where they were opened, "crime has not been a problem." Joliet [Illinois] Police Chief Joseph Beazley says the casinos in his city produce no more criminal activity than a typical discount department store.

Casinos are accused of fostering compulsive gambling, which allegedly leads to poverty, domestic abuse, divorce and suicide. But a Maryland task force that opposed legalizing casinos discounted this concern, noting in a 1995 report that the estimated number of compulsive gamblers is no higher in New Jersey, Atlantic City and all, than in Maryland. "The estimates of the social costs of pathological and problem gambling come from sources that are likely to overstate the average financial and behavioral damages experienced by persons with gambling problems," it cautioned.

Phony Calculations

Some opponents cloak their fears in supposedly incriminating economic data. The Chicago-based Better Government Association, for example, issued an absurd study claiming to prove that riverboat casinos are a net drain on the Illinois economy. Why? Because they get their revenue mostly from locals, not tourists, and send their profits to out-of-state owners. By that standard, every electronics store, movie theater, chain restaurant and automobile plant is a drain on the state economy.

Casinos, we are told, hurt local retailers by capturing dollars that used to be spent elsewhere. Sure—just like a new book store or a new art gallery. So what? If Mr. and Mrs. Smith want to spend their leisure funds playing cards at a casino instead of going out for drinks and dinner, why should we prevent them from doing that?

Lost in all the phony calculations of harm is an appreciation of the value of casinos in providing pleasure to their customers. Most patrons are not desperate gambling addicts or unwitting suckers— they're rational grownups who like to risk a few dollars on the chance of winning a few, and who think the diversion is worth the possible loss.

Some people like to bowl, some like to garden, some like to watch TV, some like to cruise the Internet, and some like to play blackjack or

Keno. It's hard to see how recreational betting is morally inferior to lots of pastimes we accept. Some people disagree, of course—and they are free to avoid it, just as teetotalers are free not to drink.

What they should not be free to do is ban it for everyone. Like any benign activity, gambling can send a few unstable sorts over the edge. But that is no reason to deprive the vast majority of people who are perfectly capable of enjoying it responsibly. Critics claim to be appalled by the specter of ruined lives. What really seems to bother them is the sight of free people making their own choices.

CHAPTER 4

INDIAN GAMING

A HISTORY OF TRIBAL GAMING

National Indian Gaming Association

In the following selection, the National Indian Gaming Association (NIGA) briefly traces the history of tribal gaming in the United States. According to the NIGA, gaming existed as a part of tribal ceremony before the arrival of Europeans in America and currently provides many tribes with much-needed revenue. Government and private interests have charged, however, that tribes should not be the sole regulators of their own gaming operations, states the NIGA. An attempt to resolve this dispute over regulation came in 1988, when Congress passed the Indian Gaming Regulatory Act (IGRA). This act, the NIGA points out, requires tribes to negotiate with states concerning gambling laws while ensuring that American Indians continue to control and benefit from reservation gaming. The NIGA is a nonprofit organization that promotes tribal gaming enterprises throughout the United States.

Gaming has been a part of the United States from the colonial era up through today. Lotteries were critical to funding the Revolutionary War and the colonization of America, and they even helped fund the beginning of venerable institutions like Harvard University and Princeton.

Indian gaming, originally part of tribal ceremonies or celebration, existed long before Europeans came to America. However, as Europeans began settling America, they gradually took away every means of self-sufficiency American Indians had: destroying agrarian societies, killing the buffalo and forcing American Indians onto remote, desolate reservations.

A Viable Source of Income

Today, gaming is often the only viable source of employment and governmental revenues available to tribes. Gaming has replaced the buffalo as the mechanism used by American Indian people for survival. The proceeds from gaming are used by Indian nations for subsistence, for cultural preservation, and for replenishing impoverished economies.

Reprinted from the National Indian Gaming Association fact sheet "The History of Tribal Gaming," as it appeared in the February 1997 issue of *Christian Social Action*, by permission of the author.

Indian gaming has been a major catalyst for community growth and economic development, generating revenues for tribes like no federal stimulus effort ever has before. After decades of poverty and high unemployment on often geographically remote reservations, Indian people now see gaming as an integral part of tribal economies and the means to achieve self-sufficiency. However, maintaining the sovereign right to conduct tribal gaming operations hasn't gone unchallenged, and opposition from state and federal governments and privately held gaming interests still grows.

Indians' Right to Conduct Gaming Operations

Large-scale gaming sponsored by tribal governments started in the early 1980s. As state lotteries began to proliferate, several Indian tribes in Florida and California began raising revenues by operating bingo games offering larger prizes than those allowed under state law. When the states threatened to close the operations, the tribes sued in federal court—*Seminole Tribe vs. Butterworth* (1979) and *California vs. Cabazon Band* (1987).

In both rulings, the courts said that if state law criminally prohibits a form of gambling, then the tribes within the state may not engage in that activity. However, if state law civilly regulates a form of gambling, then the tribes within the state may engage in that gaming free of state control. In essence, the courts formally recognized the Indians' right to conduct gaming operations on their own land as long as gaming such as bingo or "Las Vegas" nights are not criminally prohibited by the state.

In 1988, Congress formally recognized but limited the right of Indians to conduct gaming operations with the passage of the Indian Gaming Regulatory Act (IGRA). The IGRA requires tribes to negotiate with states concerning regulation while it ensures that tribal governments are the sole owners and primary beneficiaries of gaming and legislatively recognizes tribal gaming as a way of promoting economic development for tribes.

Infringing on Tribes' Rights

Since the passage of the act, states have continually challenged IGRA, not satisfied with their role in negotiating with tribes as equal sovereigns, and have demanded more regulatory control. Now, just as the tribes are beginning to build infrastructure, schools, hospitals and roads, states also demand access to the tribes' gaming revenues.

Even the National Indian Gaming Commission (NIGC), which regulates specific forms of gaming, can infringe on tribes' rights as it promulgates regulations. Over the years, several tribes have initiated court cases charging states with "bad faith" negotiation under IGRA, as well as to fight NIGC's regulations. Some have won, others lost.

Indian nations are currently meeting with members of Congress and representatives from states to address concerns and look for ways to continue an economic development tool that is benefitting Indian and non-Indian people alike.

Tribes realize that the success of gaming is not an end in itself. Rather, it is a bridge to help regain what was once theirs long ago— true self-respect, self-determination and economic self-sufficiency. Many tribes are looking beyond gaming and diversifying their economic base with other businesses. The skills and resources tribes are amassing in gaming will help assure their future and their children's future.

Indian Gaming: More at Stake than Meets the Eye

Sean Paige

Reservation gaming has benefited a few tribes, reports Sean Paige, but not all Indian-operated casinos are successful. Paige writes that the spread of tribal gaming has resulted in a rise in casino-related corruption and increased conflicts concerning Indian sovereignty, tribal leadership, and federal obligations to Native Americans. According to Paige, some argue that Indians should continue to maintain sole control over casino revenues, while others contend that tribal leaders must be required to account publicly for gambling income and to distribute casino revenues equitably among tribal members. Paige is a reporter for *Insight*, a weekly newsjournal.

For generations, Navajo elders have told and retold the Legend of the Great Gambler who, after losing everything in a high-stakes wager with the people, vows someday to return and destroy them. "Maybe the Gambler was the white man," muses Navajo chanter and medicine man Alfred Yazie, "or maybe he's coming back in the form of casinos."

Superstition or not, this story is credited by some with having led Navajos on the nation's largest reservation (in Arizona, New Mexico and Utah) to reject casino gambling in a Nov. 4, 1997, referendum, resisting pressures from tribal leaders for the second time in five years. "There is really nothing good that can come from gaming besides money," says Edison Wauneka, a tribal official who opposes casinos. "While it can make a lot of money, at the same time it's going to hurt a lot of people."

The "New Buffalo"

But apparently not every American Indian tribe shares the Navajo's chastening lore or ethical trepidations. Instead, many are betting heavily that casino gambling, called the "new buffalo" by some, will free them from the suffocating grip of federal paternalism. More than any other group of Americans, critics say Indians have reason to see the federal safety net as an entangling web from which escape is rare.

Casino-driven winds of change are sweeping through Indian country. Only days before the Navajo just said no, in a Capitol Hill hearing-room a world away from Arizona's high plateau, Interior Secretary Bruce Babbitt was denying that a $300,000 political donation from Wisconsin's Oneida tribe led him to reject a casino bid by their poorer Indian neighbors, the Chippewa.

Here was one tribe waging a big-dollar Washington lobbying campaign to block the economic development of another. Such a scenario would have seemed all but impossible a decade ago, before a 1987 Supreme Court ruling (*California vs. Cabazon Band of Mission Indians*) blazed the trail for Indian casino gaming. Few then would have predicted that the handful of reservation bingo parlors operating before 1988, when Congress passed the Indian Gaming Regulatory Act, or IGRA, in less than a decade would become a $6 billion industry with roughly 280 casinos owned by 184 tribes.

The most famous rags-to-riches story of the Indian casinos is that of Connecticut's Mashantucket Pequot tribe. Although obscure in the 1970s when only two tribal members lived on a tiny reservation, Pequots on the reservation now number more than 400 and have become an economic dynamo fueled by more than $1 billion a year in casino revenues. Another involves the once-destitute Sycuan Kummeyaay band in Southern California, each of whom today receives a reported $4,000 a month from casino "per-capitas." In a few cases—in California and Minnesota, for example—once-desolate reservations have become gated communities full of luxury homes.

These are the Cinderella stories. But while the prospects for many Indians have brightened and aspirations of others are soaring, the silver lining is not without its dark cloud.

Thus far, casinos mainly have enriched a handful of smaller tribes located near urban areas. Just eight operations account for about 40 percent of Indian casino revenues, according to the General Accounting Office (GAO). About 10 percent of the Indian casinos are losing money, experts say, though most are breaking even and a lucky few have broken the bank. Clearly, casinos aren't the answer for tribes such as the Navajo that are geographically isolated or culturally indisposed. And casino-related corruption reportedly is on the rise. Also the new economic and political muscle some tribes are flexing is raising old conflicts about land, sovereignty, money and power—not just between Indians and "the dominant culture," but among tribes themselves.

Second Thoughts on Indian Gaming

In 28 states that allow Indian gaming, tensions are mounting between governors who want more authority over casinos (and a reasonable cut of the profits) and tribes that are protective of their sovereignty, aren't required by law to divulge their finances and sometimes are operating in open defiance of state law. Tribes are confident they can win any court battle thanks to a dismal swamp of judicial decisions and jurisdictional disputes.

And some in Washington also are having second thoughts. The $13.8 billion Interior Department appropriations bill, signed at the end of 1997, established a one-year moratorium on any new tribal gambling compacts not already approved by states. Wyoming Republican Sen. Mike Enzi, who offered the amendment, hopes the pause will give the National Gambling Impacts Study Commission time to complete a review of gaming's economic and cultural consequences. Enzi also wants to include feedback from non-Indians and give states more leverage in negotiating gaming compacts with tribes. "Gambling deals have no place being struck without the approval of the people on and off the reservations. The effects of gambling don't stop at the tribal border," says Enzi, pointing to studies showing that $3 in costs are created for every $1 in tax revenues that gambling generates.

House Ways and Means Committee Chairman Bill Archer of Texas and House Rules Committee Chairman Gerald Solomon of New York are grumbling that profitable tribal casinos should pay federal taxes just as non-Indian casinos do. Tribes currently pay no federal taxes on income made on tribal land, no state income taxes on income earned on the reservation, no sales taxes on transactions on the reservation and no local property taxes on Indian trust or reservation lands.

An Archer proposal to tax Indian gaming revenues as part of the balanced-budget negotiations was voted down but someday may be revisited, according to Capitol Hill sources. That would betray "solemn obligations" of the United States, says Arizona Republican Sen. John McCain. "We took all the rest of their land and we guaranteed them certain things," he contends. "Sometimes the impact of those treaties has not been as pleasant as we want them to be, and taxing is just one of those things."

Corruption on Indian Reservations

Corruption on Indian reservations may be exacerbated by the presence of casinos, say critics. Fred Dakota, former tribal chairman of Michigan's Keweenaw Bay Indians, recently was sentenced to two years in prison for taking kickbacks from a slot-machine company. Dakota, who was known as the father of tribal gaming for opening one of the nation's first Indian casinos in his two-car garage, is one of many tribal officials caught up in casino-related corruption.

In 1996, the GAO reported that the rapid growth of legalized gambling enterprises nationwide, and relatively loose regulation of those on reservations, made the operations susceptible to money laundering. Yet the Indian Gaming Commission employs only six investigators to monitor roughly 280 casinos, respond to hot-line tips, issue violation notices and conduct background investigations of non-

Indian casino contractors.

Then there is the new litigiousness about unresolved questions concerning old treaties and tribal sovereignty. Claiming that treaties entitle them to half of the clam and oyster harvest on Puget Sound, tribes in Washington state have sued for the right to harvest on what is now private property. Cortez, Colo., truck-stop owner Mark Larson was brought before the state's Civil Rights Commission for failing to accept checks from Utes living on a nearby reservation—a policy he enacted because the truck stop was unable through tribal courts to collect on bad checks. And many service stations near reservations are being driven out of business, according to the Society of Independent Gasoline Marketers of America, because they can't compete with nearby, tax-exempt, tribally owned business.

The New Tribal Assertiveness

Some observers fear that the new tribal assertiveness is inviting a backlash, while others contend the clashes are a welcome sign of Indian economic emergence. "I think the issues are becoming much more difficult to deal with," says Colorado Republican Sen. Ben Nighthorse Campbell, the only American Indian in Congress and the first ever to chair the Senate Indian Affairs Committee. "And as tribes build political clout—and they are now learning how to use the system everybody else has used for years—it becomes much more difficult to find a solution when nobody wants to give." Some tribes formerly content to maintain their sovereignty and slice of the federal pie are becoming more assertive, even "expansionist," Campbell says.

With "over 100 new casinos now on the drawing boards," Campbell worries that the United States soon will reach a "saturation point" when "tribe will be turning against tribe. In some communities where the casinos have made some Indians the new rich, a backlash has been created"—especially when non-Indians see their federal tax dollars going to rich tribes.

The tumult is a harbinger of a better tomorrow, says W. Ron Allen, president of the National Congress of American Indians, or NCAI, the leading advocacy organization for tribal governments. "There's tension, no question about it," he asserts. "The fact that tribes are stronger and more effective causes some annoyance. Tribes now are becoming effective players, and [non-Indians] have to deal with that."

Confronting Gaming Mania

One Indian confronting the dark side of casino mania head-on is Bill Lawrence of Bemidji, Minn., a member of the Red Lake band of Chippewas and publisher of the *Native American Press/Ojibwe News*. The former Marine likens conditions on some reservations to those in the former Soviet Union, where Indians and non-Indians alike have few rights and anyone challenging corrupt tribal leaders risks losing their job and housing or might land in jail. And casino revenues aren't making the situation any more democratic.

"The Navajo voted [gambling] down again. The Hopi voted it down. But tribes in Minnesota have never had an opportunity to vote on it at all," says Lawrence. "Had we had that opportunity we probably would have put safeguards in place. We have no accountability. We don't know where the money goes, and there's no way we can force our elected officials to account to us."

Voting the leadership out isn't easy, he explains. "They have the checkbook and they can buy the best attorneys, they can buy the best lobbyists, they can buy anything."

For running investigative stories that have helped put eight state tribal leaders behind bars, Lawrence's newspaper has been boycotted by tribal casinos and his wife fired from a teaching job at a tribal school. He's been derided as an "Indian Uncle Tom." One leader Lawrence helped send to jail called him "a crab at the bottom of the pot," saying, "Every time somebody tries to crawl out, he's there to pull them back in."

But Lawrence seems less interested in who crawls out than in how they do it and who they crawl over along the way. "The biggest abusers and exploiters of Indians are other Indian people," says Lawrence, who believes reservations won't become more democratic or tribal leaders more accountable until they no longer can hide behind claims of absolute sovereignty. "You have to pierce the veil; they can't have this absolute control," Lawrence says of tribal leaders. "They've been hiding their criminal conduct behind it for years."

He recommends that the Indian Civil Rights Act of 1968 be amended to allow Indians and non-Indians alike to take tribes and tribally owned companies to court, which is not permitted now, and amend the Indian Gaming Act so that tribes must account publicly for casino revenues. But that will be difficult, Lawrence acknowledges, given the growing lobbying power of tribes and the "noble-savage mentality of too many of the senators and Eastern people that these tribes can do nothing wrong."

In the meantime, Lawrence has established the nonprofit Tribal Accountability Legal Rights Fund to help Indians and non-Indians get justice in tribal courts.

Challenging Indian Sovereignty

One member of Congress who has dared to "pierce the veil" of the Indian sovereignty issue is Sen. Slade Gorton, a Washington Republican. Gorton, whose involvement with Indian issues dates to his days as the Evergreen State's attorney general, failed to add amendments to the Interior Department appropriations bill that would have waived tribal immunity from civil lawsuits and means-test wealthy tribes to ensure that federal payments go to those most in need.

The more Gorton learned about Indian law as state attorney general, "the more anachronistic a system of dual sovereignty seemed," he says. "My fundamental view then and my fundamental view now is that all Americans ought to be treated equally under the law." Recently Gorton's interest was drawn by a case in which an Indian police officer killed a teenager in an auto accident but avoided a lawsuit by invoking tribal immunity.

"Slade Gorton says tribal governments are an anachronism in today's society," responds Allen of the NCAI. "We argue that his thinking, which is a conquest thinking, is an anachronism because we believe our society is much more sophisticated than that."

Gorton also is asking questions about federal obligations under Indian treaties signed during the 1800s, most of which he believes were not open-ended, and whether Tribal Priority Allocations of money are fairly distributed. "There is a question as to whether there is an obligation by the people of the United States to support Indian tribal government in perpetuity," says Gorton. "It is absolutely clear, however, that there is no such treaty right. The treaties, almost without exception, talk about support for 15 or 20 years."

The federal government signed 350 Indian treaties between 1778 and 1871, when Congress stopped the practice. Another 45 treaties were negotiated but never ratified. The treaties "often contain obsolete commitments which either have been fulfilled or superseded by congressional legislation," according to the World Wide Web site of the Bureau of Indian Affairs, or BIA, which acknowledges that "the provision of education, health, welfare and other services by the government often has been extended beyond treaty requirements."

"Assuming any given level of support, shouldn't we then have a rationale under which those tribes that have the least ability to raise money for themselves get the greatest degree of financial support?" Gorton asks. "My fundamental philosophy is that [tribes] want the right of self-determination, and I don't quarrel with that. However, I think the right to self-determination carries with it an implied duty of self-support."

Gorton believes his amendments received little backing "because people are afraid to be called the kinds of names some people are calling me." But in defeat he won a pledge by the Senate Indian Affairs Committee to hold public hearings on these issues in the spring of 1998 and a GAO study of how tribal monies are distributed.

In seeking the study, Gorton may have had in mind the case of housing officials on Washington state's Tululip Indian reservation who used low-income housing grants from the Department of Housing and Urban Development, or HUD, to build themselves $300,000 luxury homes. Or that of the Pequot tribe which, in spite of making $1 million a day in casino revenues, still received $1.5 million in low-income housing assistance in 1996. Or Arizona's Fort McDowell Apaches, each of whom receives an average of $3,000 a month in profit-sharing, who sold off 64 federally funded housing units for $1 each.

Will Gaming Promote Economic Development?

Sudden wealth has not sated the strong sense of entitlement of some tribes. Minnesota's Fond du Lac Chippewas voted against spending $9 million to replace a dilapidated school even though the tribe had $30 million in banked casino revenues. "The United States has an obligation to Indian people, and I'm going to hold them to it," the tribe's chairman told the Minneapolis *Star Tribune* recently. Even if the tribe has money enough to pay for it themselves? "Does Bob Hope need Social Security?" the chairman asks rhetorically. "He's eligible for it."

Critics argue that lasting economic development for Indians won't be possible until the wreckage of the Indian welfare state is jettisoned. Proof of its overwhelming failure is plain to both left and right. Reservation housing remains in shambles despite $4.3 billion in federal housing assistance during the last decade. More than 100,000 American Indians are believed to be homeless or living in substandard housing. About 73 percent of the 1.2 million Indians on or near the nation's 275 Indian reservations earn less than $9,000 a year, well below the poverty level. And Indian unemployment continues to hover at about 50 percent.

First on nearly everyone's list for reform is the BIA, which will spend $1.7 billion on Indian programs and direct payments in 1998. "BIA is the greatest detriment to economic development on Indian reservations," says McCain. "If you want to set up a business in Flagstaff, Ariz., it takes two or three days. If you go up to Window Rock, which is the capital of the Navajo Nation, it takes between two and three years to start a business because of a 32-step process."

"Gaming, in my view, is not going to be a long-term solution," McCain continues. "Those tribes that have signed self-governing pacts [assigning themselves the responsibility for administering programs] are uniformly doing better than they were under the Bureau of Indian Affairs."

But what confidence can taxpayers have that tribal governments are going to be any more competent than the bumbling BIA? "If tribal leaders don't govern responsibly they can be voted out," McCain says, "but you can never vote out a BIA bureaucrat."

"There's always been a love-hate relationship between Indians and the BIA," adds Campbell, who blames much of the BIA problems on Indian hiring preferences. "The bureau is the only agency in the federal government that *can* discriminate. They can hire Indian preference before anybody else. I think it should be done away with. There are some very, very good people in the bureau, but there also are some very bad ones who got in there and have worked their way into key positions without having the management skills to be able to do the job."

Public Policy and Indian Leadership

BIA spokesman Thomas Sweeney maintains that the agency doesn't deserve to be the whipping boy. He says that 90 percent of BIA's money is delivered directly to tribes, its tasks are complicated and jurisdictions far-flung, and instead blames much of the problem on vacillating government policies. "Indian policy has shifted tremendously over a long period of time," he says. "The BIA has to respond to many shifts of direction."

Meanwhile, Indian leadership has been stymied by the old system. "Right now, with the BIA running everything, these are tribal leaders in name only," McCain says, "and there's no responsibility and accountability."

"Public policy has to give Indians the opportunity to show leadership," says Peter Ferrara, who is writing a book on the subject with Philip Martin, leader of the highly successful Mississippi Choctaws, whose economic empowerment predated casinos. Martin, often viewed as a model tribal leader, years ago recognized that Indian reservations can be enterprise zones and today is a vigorous defender of free markets.

"The federal government has to say to Indians, 'We're moving out, it's time for you to take over,'" Ferrara says, which will "open up the opportunity for leadership."

Yet it is the Navajo leadership that is pressuring its more traditional constituents to disregard ancient teachings and embrace gaming, with all its attendant problems. "It was the leaders that pushed this gaming issue onto us," says Navajo tribal official Wauneka, "and it's already been stated that even though the people voted no in this referendum, the Navajo Nation council still has the ultimate authority and can on their own approve gaming on the Navajo Nation."

But for Wauneka the choice remains as plain and stark as the Arizona landscape. "You really have to determine what is good and what is wrong," he says. "And gaming is on the wrong."

THE PEQUOTS HAVE BENEFITED FROM RESERVATION GAMING

G. Michael Brown

Gaming has benefited the Mashantucket Pequot tribe of southern Connecticut, G. Michael Brown argues in the following selection. The 1992 opening—and ensuing expansion—of Foxwoods Casino on the Pequot reservation created thousands of jobs and helped to offset the potentially damaging effects of factory and industry layoffs in Connecticut, Brown maintains. Furthermore, he reports, casino revenues now give Pequots access to high-quality housing, education, job training, and medical care. Brown is the president and chief executive officer of Foxwoods Casino in Ledyard, Connecticut.

Home to less than 300 tribal members, the reservation of the Mashantucket Pequot tribe is located on about 4,000 acres of land in southeastern Connecticut, 45 miles east of Hartford, the state capital.

Like many smaller tribes throughout the United States, the Mashantucket Pequots often resorted to small, high-risk enterprises to improve their economic well-being. Among these enterprises were a small sand and gravel operation, a maple syrup-production facility, a restaurant, and even hydroponic lettuce cultivation. Most tribal members, however, worked as laborers in nearby factories.

Moreover, like other tribes, the Pequots also vied for federal grants to aid their efforts in upgrading education, medical care, and housing. Tribal housing, in fact, consisted of 35 homes and apartments financed by the U.S. Department of Housing and Urban Department.

The Origin of Foxwoods

For as long as anyone could remember, the tribe's future looked bleak. Indeed, banks were reluctant to lend the tribe money; jobs—especially good-paying jobs—were scarce; and the Pequots' small numbers made it difficult for them to compete against larger tribes for federal monies. From his small office located in a converted house trailer, Pequot Chairman Richard (Skip) Hayward worked diligently to convince tribe members who had left to return home. His efforts to repa-

Reprinted from G. Michael Brown, "In New England," *Forum for Applied Research and Public Policy*, Summer 1996, by permission of the publisher.

triate his tribe were compromised because he had little to offer members for their return to the reservation.

Then, on Independence Day weekend in 1986, the Pequots' fortunes changed when they opened a bingo hall financed by a $4-million loan from the Arab American Bank that was guaranteed by the Bureau of Indian Affairs. The tribe also received administrative help from members of the Penobscot Tribe, who had acquired valuable experience in operating a bingo hall on their reservation in Maine.

By 1988, just two years later, the Pequots had paid off their loan (two years ahead of schedule) and assumed full responsibility for the management of the facility. That same year, the bingo hall earned $14 million.

It was in 1988 that the federal government also passed the Indian Gaming Regulatory Act. That law gave Indian tribes the right to sponsor casino gaming on their reservations if they were located within a state that "allowed gaming by any person for any purpose." Four years later, the state of Connecticut and the Pequots signed a compact leading to the opening of Foxwoods Casino Resorts on February 15, 1992.

According to the terms of the compact, the state's Tribal Gaming Commission was granted a substantial role in licensing and regulating gaming on the reservation. Employees of Connecticut's Liquor Control, Division of Special Revenue, and state police were stationed on Foxwoods' property 24 hours a day, seven days a week, and the Pequots were obligated to pay all costs associated with state law enforcement and regulation taking place on the reservation.

The Pequots, in return, were given the right to establish a casino-based enterprise on their reservation. To insure the integrity of the operation, the tribe hired the nation's most experienced regulators and managers, including Robert Winter, former director of the state of New Jersey's Division of Criminal Justice, and George Henningsen, former chief of the division's Organized Crime Special Prosecution Section.

New Jobs and Earnings

Foxwoods' arrival couldn't have come at a better time. The day that Foxwoods opened its doors, with a staff of 2,300 people, General Dynamics' Electric Boat Division headquartered in nearby Groton, Connecticut, announced that it was laying off 2,000 people.

Foxwoods' original facility consisted of 40,000 square feet of gaming space with 125 tables, one gourmet restaurant, a buffet, and a grill/coffee shop. Expansion began just 10 days after the resort opened.

Today, the complex consists of a poker room, bingo hall, more than 275 table games, nearly 4,000 slot machines (the original facility had none), a food court, a large theater for live performances, a cinema complex, and two hotels. All together, Foxwoods has nearly 275,000 square feet of gaming space, 12,000 square feet of retail space, nearly 600 hotel rooms, and 12 restaurants that serve an average of 17,000 meals a day.

The company currently employs 10,500 people who cater to the needs of an average of 55,000 visitors per day—that's 20 million people per year. Another 1,000 people work for the Pequot's tribal government or are employed with state regulatory or enforcement agencies whose salaries are paid for by the Pequots.

In 1995, Foxwoods' payroll exceeded $260 million. In addition, the company's employee benefit package includes free medical and eyecare; disability insurance; paid sick and vacation time; and a 401-K pension plan. The company also gives employees free meals.

Foxwoods' employees pay property tax, state and federal income tax, and sales taxes. In fact, the company's contributions to the federal government's social-security and medicare coffers topped $15 million in 1995; employees matched that amount raising the total contribution to more than $30 million.

As Arthur W. Wright, professor of economics at the University of Connecticut, recently noted: "The startling growth of Foxwoods Casino . . . has [brought] new jobs and earnings . . . to a state racked by recession and defense cuts since 1989."

In fact, Wright concludes that Foxwoods is ultimately responsible for an additional 30,000 jobs throughout the state. More than 10,000 of these jobs have been generated through direct hires. Nearly twice that many have resulted from Foxwoods' capital investments and employee spending. These new jobs have added an estimated $600 million to the state's payroll each year over the past several years.

As the November 7, 1994, edition of *U.S. News & World Report* notes:

> Connecticut has been staggered by setbacks in defense and insurance, two of its most important industries. Military costs have contributed to the state's loss of 13.3 percent of its manufacturing jobs. Insurers have seen profits wrecked by a string of national disasters and industry consolidation. Insurance employment in the state has fallen by nearly 11,000 jobs since 1991. This decline hasn't helped commercial real estate. Connecticut is having trouble attracting new growth engines. The state ranks last in business start-ups, and the only large-scale job growth has taken place at Foxwoods Resort Casino, which has added 10,000 positions since 1992. Without Foxwoods, Connecticut would have had no job growth over the past [few] years.

Benefits for the Pequot Tribe

Foxwoods is now the largest single contributor to Connecticut's state budget, exceeding the contributions made by the previous bulwarks of the state's economy—the defense and insurance industries.

Yet, the benefits that Foxwoods provides the state far exceed its contributions to local, state, and federal government coffers. First, the lives of tribal members, particularly Pequots' elders, have improved considerably. Housing, education, and medical care, which historically have been substandard, now exceed national standards. Facilities and services, moreover, no longer require subsidies from federal and state government agencies. For example, 75 single-family homes have been built under a tribal-sponsored housing program that allows tribal members to obtain low-interest mortgages.

In addition, the tribe provides comprehensive training and placement services for its members. This program offers members the opportunity to learn valuable job skills that will help them secure a bright future—often with Foxwoods. Some 23 Pequot tribal members are now enrolled in this program.

Another 35 tribal members, who are enrolled as full-time college students, don't pay a cent for their education, compliments of their tribal government. Still another 25 members are earning their high-school equivalency diplomas, without spending any money of their own. They have benefitted from stipends offered by the tribal government to advance their education.

The Pequots also have tried to diversify their business portfolios beyond gaming. For example, the tribal government has purchased Randall's Ordinary, a specialty restaurant, and Norwich Inn & Spa, an upscale inn consisting of 100 deluxe rooms, 205 villas and 7 meeting rooms, and, as the name suggests, a spa. Both the restaurant and inn are located in Connecticut towns near the reservation.

The tribe also has established a tribal court, which initially handled only casino tort cases but now covers virtually all legal matters within the reservation. The tribe also has organized a state-of-the-art tribal police department and fire and emergency-medical service departments.

The tribal court and its police, fire, and emergency-medical service departments offer additional employment opportunities for tribal members and bring an added element of justice and security to the reservation.

Moreover, the tribe is now constructing a multi-million dollar museum and cultural resource center. Not only will the history and culture of the Pequots be preserved through this facility, but millions of visitors who come to the reservation each year will learn a great deal about the history of the tribe.

Gaining Independence Through Games of Chance

The revenues generated through gaming have enabled the Pequots to help their own tribal members, the local community, the state of Connecticut, and the nation as a whole. In 1995, for example, the tribe donated $10 million to the Smithsonian Institute and $2 million to the Special Olympics.

All told, 126 Indian tribes in 24 states across the nation have negotiated 141 compacts to operate legalized casino gaming. Minnesota boasts 17 tribal gaming facilities that employ nearly 10,000 people, making Indian casinos the state's seventh largest employer. Wisconsin tribes operate 15 gaming facilities, and Michigan tribes operate 11; each employ about 7,000 people. Tribes in Arizona, California, New York, Mississippi, and Washington also have joined the gaming industry.

These enterprises have generated jobs and taxes that help drive their states' economies. In many states, including Connecticut, tribal gaming enterprises have provided the only source of economic growth over the past few years. As a result, such enterprises have helped stabilize troubled economies rocked by factory closings and industry layoffs.

It is indeed ironic that games of chance have become one of the few sure bets for local and state economies and that American Indian tribes, which have depended on government monies for their well being in the past, have gained independence through the bingo halls, casinos, and slot machines that they now own and operate.

CASINOS DO NOT HELP MOST NATIVE AMERICANS

Ben Nighthorse Campbell

According to Ben Nighthorse Campbell, Republican senator from Colorado, the majority of Native Americans derive no economic benefit from reservation gaming. He points out that the few tribes that offer gaming often fail to generate revenues because of restrictive state regulations or the reservation's remoteness from populated areas. Other means of building tribal economies, such as investment in small non-gaming businesses, deserve support from private and public agencies, Campbell concludes.

The phenomenal success of the Foxwoods casino in Ledyard, Conn., has led many Americans to believe that gambling is an economic panacea for Native Americans. Nothing could be further from the truth.

According to the 1990 census, Native Americans are the nation's poorest group; 31 percent live below the poverty level. In the 1980's, their average household income fell by 5 percent, while that of all other major racial and ethnic groups rose. The average annual income of Native Americans living on reservations is less than $5,000.

Gambling will not quickly improve these grim statistics. Of the more than 500 U.S. tribes, fewer than 100 have casino-type operations. And most casinos cannot make huge profits because of their small size, isolation and state restrictions.

Many Factors Hamper Gaming Success

Consider the Fort Peck reservation, in northeastern Montana, which has a 70 percent unemployment rate although its Assiniboines and Sioux are considered high-stakes gambling tribes. Their operations are hampered by the state's prohibition on slot machines and blackjack games.

Foxwoods, run by the Mashantucket Pequots, is expected to generate more than half a billion dollars from slot machines alone in 1995. At 200,000 square feet, the casino contains more square feet than the total of all the homes and businesses on many reservations.

Tribes need outside investors to raise the millions of dollars needed

From Ben Nighthorse Campbell, "The Foxwoods Myth," *The New York Times*, March 29, 1995. Copyright ©1995 by The New York Times Company. Reprinted by permission.

to build large casinos. Potential speculators will be interested if the reservations are close to a large population and far from competitors. Foxwoods is the only casino in one of the country's wealthiest and most densely populated areas. But in Alaska, home to 85,000 Native Americans, 80 percent of the villages cannot be reached by roads. Navajos in Chinle, Ariz., must drive 70 miles across the reservation to reach a bank.

Building Tribal Economies

The condition of Indian lands can keep investors away. After years of neglect, reservations often lack running water, sewers and trash disposal. Yet the situation is far from hopeless. With the support of investors, Federal money and private donors, many tribes are building economies.

In Browning, Mont., the Blackfeet used oil and gas revenues to buy an insolvent local bank in 1987. This Government-insured institution attracts deposits from charitable organizations, corporations and other tribes. It gives loans to Indians and others on the reservation.

On the Pine Ridge Reservation in South Dakota (in the nation's poorest county), the Lakota Fund invests in small enterprises such as video rental stores, auto mechanic shops and manufacturers of traditional crafts.

There are 29 tribal colleges across the nation, including one run by my own tribe, the Northern Cheyenne. According to the most recent data from the American Council on Education, in 1991 almost 14,000 Indians were enrolled in these schools, up from 2,100 in 1982.

Many Still Need Help

As they build local economies, these tribes bring down unemployment rates, reduce welfare rolls and earn the respect of neighboring communities. We should applaud those that have found routes out of poverty through casinos or other means. But just because a small percentage of tribes can make it through gambling, private donors and public agencies should not abandon the less fortunate reservations.

THE YAVAPAI PEOPLE HIT THE JACKPOT

Elizabeth Manning

A 1992 confrontation between the federal government and the Yavapai tribe over the lawfulness of reservation gaming resulted in negotiations that legalized casinos on Indian land in Arizona, Elizabeth Manning reports. Casino revenue has enabled the Yavapai to distribute per capita payments among its members; it has also prompted the building of new homes and healthy investment in non-gaming businesses, Manning writes. However, she maintains, the tribe has had to contend with the financial irresponsibility of some of its members as well as the nation's recent backlash against gambling. Manning is a former staff reporter for the *High Country News*, a biweekly journal that focuses on issues of interest in the western region of the United States.

It started as a traditional cowboy and Indian battle—one the Indians were supposed to lose. At 6:00 on a May morning in 1992, a team of FBI agents accompanied by eight Mayflower moving vans invaded the Fort McDowell Reservation in Arizona. Armed agents broke into the tribal bingo hall and began carting slot machines into the vans. SWAT teams set up guard on the roof.

By then the Indian telephone network was awake and at work. The first calls came from tribal members at the hall. From neighbor to cousin to friend to the media, the message spread: Come down to the gaming center and bring a car or pickup. By the time the vans were ready to roll, the Indians had hemmed in the 18-wheelers with heavy machinery and dozens of vehicles, including the tribe's small fleet of sand and gravel trucks. More seriously, the FBI agents faced a thoroughly awake and angry Yavapai Nation.

As the Indians saw it, this was sovereign land and the FBI was stealing the only dependable livelihood they had managed to find in a century of white rule. Tribal president Clinton Pattea recalls, "After they loaded the trucks, our people blocked the entrance. It was a rather scary situation. They came in without any notice."

Reprinted from Elizabeth Manning, "Gambling: A Tribe Hits the Jackpot," *High Country News*, April 1, 1996, by permission of the publisher.

"It was lucky for them we're not a violent tribe," says tribal member Nimrod Thomas.

Given the sudden confrontation, anything could have happened. What did happen was the arrival several hours later by helicopter of Arizona Gov. Fife Symington, the toughest-talking and most pugnacious governor in the West. Whether Symington knew it or not, he was coming to negotiate his unconditional surrender.

Civil disobedience appeared to be the only option the tribe had. Pattea says he and other Indian leaders had been trying for years to meet with an Arizona governor to start negotiations over the slot machines. Negotiations were required under a 1988 federal law sanctioning Indian gaming, but the tribes' advances had been rejected by former Govs. Rose Moffort, Evan Mecham, and finally Symington. If the vans left with the slot machines, the tribe would have lost all leverage.

The confrontation must have shaken the governor. Four other raids on Indian casinos that morning had gone well for the FBI. Then he heard of the Yavapai blockade. Fearing violence or a forced agreement less to his liking, Symington started talking.

Within an hour and a half, he and Pattea had worked out a temporary standoff: The slot machines would stay in the vans, but the vans would stay in the gaming center parking lot pending further negotiations. In the following weeks, Arizona's tribes staged powwows next to the vans while the machines baked under the desert sun. Public sympathy swelled.

The Benefits of Legal Gaming

A little more than a year later, the Fort McDowell Yavapai tribe had a 10-year compact with Symington and a fully legal and open casino. By April 1994, Symington had signed similar compacts with 16 of Arizona's 21 tribes. Phoenix is now ringed by three casinos; 12 others are spread across the state.

"They were a great example for all the tribes in the nation," says Carolina Butler, 61, who helped the Yavapai fight an earlier battle against a dam that would have flooded part of the reservation. "And they're a tiny tribe. Immediately, you see David and Goliath. It's so easy to roll over you when you're tiny."

It's not so easy to roll over the Fort McDowell Yavapai now, says Butler, a Mesa resident who describes herself as a "Mexican-American housewife turned activist." She says she's seen the tribe develop from not knowing how to send a telegram in 1972 to running a multimillion dollar business in 1996.

The casino's earning power has exceeded the tribe's wildest expectations. Though Pattea won't reveal the tribe's exact profit, he offers a ballpark figure of $100 million annually. "It's been tremendous," he says.

The money allows the tribe to give each adult of the 850-member tribe an annual income of $36,000 plus free medical and dental insurance. If the casino continues to prosper, young children in school today will receive a trust fund of up to $500,000 when they graduate from high school; high school dropouts don't get the money until they turn 21.

The tribe has also aggressively weaned itself from dependence on outside governments. Tribal members no longer take welfare from federal, state or county governments. And the federal Bureau of Indian Affairs—with its social workers, housing programs and natural resource advisors—is mostly gone.

Even as it provides income and services for its members, the tribe earmarks 30 percent of its earnings for future economic development. The investment is required under the 1988 Indian Gaming Regulatory Act, but Pattea also knows it's important insurance for the future.

Gov. Symington makes no secret of his contempt for the Indian casinos. When the Salt River Pima-Maricopa tribe, Fort McDowell's neighbor to the southwest, tried to negotiate a compact in the spring of 1995, Symington announced he would refuse any new compacts. The tribe is crying discrimination, but Lisa Hauser, counsel to the governor, says it was just the luck of the draw. Salt River was the first tribe to approach the governor after a 9th Circuit Court of Appeals case permitted California to forbid slot machines on Indian lands, says Hauser. The ruling is not the last legal word, but it does give Symington a temporary edge.

Symington's unequivocal goal is to phase out Indian gaming as the existing compacts expire. "Native Americans have a monopoly right now," he says. "They have 10 years to profit from that monopoly. Then it comes to an end."

The Casino

It's hard to imagine "The Fort" standing empty. Open 24 hours a day, seven days a week, this enormous casino is never silent. Even at 8 a.m., slot machines blink, beep and clink as early-morning and late-night gamblers carry cottage cheese containers full of coins around the cavernous slot room, scouting a lucky machine. The line for the $2.95 breakfast buffet stretches almost into the 1,600-seat bingo hall.

The tribe reports that every day some 10,000 customers try their luck here at bingo, poker, slot machines, live keno or off-track betting on greyhound races. Each week, the tribe nets $1.5 million to $2 million from gamblers' losses.

"Location is everything," say real estate agents, and Fort McDowell has it. Only 23 miles northeast of downtown, it's the closest of the three Phoenix-area casinos. This one gets an extra boost from the large number of "snowbirds" that roost in the sunbelt; retirees fill the casino during the day while younger patrons are off at work.

Outside the casino, it's relatively quiet. The casino is at the south-ernmost end of this skinny 25,000-acre reservation that runs in a strip along the Verde River. The parking lot affords a panoramic view of Four Peaks, Red Mountain and the Superstition Mountains, all home to the *Kakakas,* or little people, who protect the Yavapai. Subdivisions spreading east from Scottsdale into the Sonoran desert end abruptly at the reservation's border; the tribal land is wilder, less manicured.

"The Fort" didn't just spring up suddenly among the mesquite bosques. With the help of a management firm that provided the investment money and expertise, the casino started modestly as a high-stakes bingo hall in 1984, says Mona Nuñez, a tribal member who heads personnel for the casino. The tribe could have sat back and let the management firm run the show for a 30 percent take of the casino's profits. But it wanted the added revenue and expertise of run-ning a business, so in 1990 it bought out the management contract.

After doubling the size of the bingo hall, the tribe decided to bring in the now-famous slot machines. They were actually video poker and bingo machines, says Nuñez, and the tribe decided they were "Class II" machines and not subject to state jurisdiction. The Indian Gaming Commission, however, ruled that they were "Class III"—the type states regulate. That's when the FBI raided.

A Large Business

Since the governor signed Fort McDowell's compact, the tribe has expanded twice, more than tripling the casino's size. Completed in 1994, this is the building that stands today. Now it has 475 slot machines, more than 70 poker tables and a 300-seat restaurant.

As Fort McDowell has grown bigger, so has its purchasing power. Businesses come to the reservation now, seeking contracts for every-thing from the satin jackets sold in the gift shop to office furniture and bingo cards. "They visit us just like they would a factory outlet center," says Nuñez.

The casino has become one of the area's largest businesses, employ-ing 1,300 workers, most of whom commute from nearby cities like Phoenix, Mesa, Fountain Hills, Scottsdale and others. It takes a mix of talent to run a casino: everything from skilled accountants, managers, slot technicians and poker dealers to minimum-wage food servers and money changers.

Most positions pay average casino wages, starting at $4.25 an hour plus medical benefits and a pension fund. It may not sound like much, but many employees say they were underemployed before.

"For five years, I had a 'roach coach.' I sold lunches at the Mayo Clinic (in Scottsdale) and at construction sites," says Sherry Williams, assistant food and beverage manager for the casino. "They treat us well here."

The casino has meant new careers for some. Tribal member Eric

Dorchester works in the casino's computer division. He maintains the network and develops programs specific to the casino's needs.

"Before, all I knew about computers is it's a box," says Dorchester, who used to work as a pipe fitter for a gas company. "To me, it's playing. I don't have to get down on my knees." His daughters now play computer games at home on an old unit discarded by the casino.

But most community members have little to do with the daily operations of the casino. Nuñez says many members quit their casino jobs when per capita payments began in 1994. The latest wave of resignations came in October 1995, she says, when the payments became monthly rather than quarterly. Overall, tribal employment at the casino dropped from 68 to 22.

A Double-Edged Sword

The per capita payments have proved a double-edged sword. Roughly half of the tribe has put the money to good use, estimates Dolly Brudevold, director of Behavior Health Services for the tribe. The other half is in trouble.

The more successful money managers are educated tribal members who are accustomed to working, she says. Those people have bought a new car or taken a family trip. But they are also looking ahead and investing, realizing the money probably won't last forever. Some went through a brief "fantasy of free spending" and are now becoming financially responsible. Many are taking advantage of financial management seminars offered by the tribe.

It's the bottom half of the tribe Brudevold worries about. These tribal members typically haven't held jobs and many have problems with addiction to drugs or alcohol. For them, the money hasn't changed anything, except perhaps the magnitude of their mistakes.

Unfortunately, the people who need the most help are also the most difficult to reach, says Brudevold. Tight family networks have kept the tribe together through poverty and adverse times such as the FBI raid, but they also make tribal members wary of telling their problems to outsiders.

"The per capita payments were probably done prematurely," she says. "We didn't have a chance to stabilize some of the social ills."

Now the tribe is playing catch-up. Brudevold says the tribe has had to protect the financial accounts of some elderly members whose children were stealing from them. It also sometimes deducts the cost of foster care from the monthly checks of irresponsible parents.

"When you have a community of people not used to the luxury of a steady income and large sums of money, you create some distortions of what wealth is and how to use it," she adds.

That threat of distortion looms largest for young people. With more than 50 percent of the tribe's population under 18, how they react to the money will determine the community's future. The short-term results haven't been encouraging, says Brudevold: The high school drop-out rate rose by 20 percent after per capita payments began.

She predicts those numbers will stabilize soon, as the tribe develops more programs to help youth, such as the first junior rodeo, held in March 1996 at the tribe's new 4,000-seat arena.

And at least the money is there now for college, says Pattea. "Before, we had a difficult time sending our kids to college."

Money for Community Services

In addition to direct payments to individuals, the tribe has put roughly another third of the money into services and community buildings. With 230 people employed by the tribal government (compared to 15 in 1960), the tribe now has the means to help nearly anyone who wants it, says Pattea. That has meant taking over services formerly provided by federal agencies such as the Bureau of Indian Affairs and Indian Health Services. The tribe is also constructing new buildings to house those services; some $24.5 million has already been spent or set aside for community improvements such as a gym, a healing center, a preschool, a health center, and water and sewer lines for the reservation.

Over the next few years the tribe will also build some 60 new homes for its families. The tribe owns the homes and rents them for $100 to $300, just enough to cover maintenance, says Pattea. These aren't the box-like homes built previously by Housing and Urban Development. The new pink stucco three- to five-bedroom homes with red tile roofs look like the ones in neighboring Fountain Hills, a swishy desert subdivision whose claim to fame is a gushing fountain as tall as the Washington Monument.

The irony of the Yavapai constructing upscale new homes is not lost on Mona Nuñez. She says Fountain Hills was planned here because the developer thought Orme Dam, which would have buried most of the tribe's land under water, was a sure bet. Fountain Hills was designed to sit alongside a lake, rather than next to a reservation.

Charlotte and Gordon Roehrig moved into one of the tribe's new homes in the Christmas of 1995. They had been living in a cramped Mesa apartment because of substandard housing on the reservation. "It's a dream, you know, getting a new home and being able to say its yours," says Charlotte Roehrig.

Finally, with another 30 percent of the money, the tribe is looking to the future—to the days when gambling might be illegal, or legal everywhere in Arizona. The tribe has built a new gas station along the highway and strengthened its existing sand and gravel operation. It is also planning to plant 1,500 acres of pecan, walnut and citrus trees, says Pattea.

Tribal leaders are also considering building a small shopping center, a golf course, water park, convenience store and possibly even a destination resort. And if by some chance gambling does become legal throughout the state, adds Pattea, the tribe might buy a casino in downtown Phoenix.

A Grand Experiment

Relying on gambling for this grand experiment in self-sufficiency has its risks. Even if Indian gambling in Arizona escapes a gubernatorial clamp-down, another more widespread threat looms over the tribe's new prosperity.

Anti-gambling forces are convincing more and more Americans that the social ills associated with the industry aren't worth the benefits—even for Indian communities.

It's happened twice before, says gambling scholar I. Nelson Rose. The nation's first era of widespread gambling ended with the spread of Jacksonian morality, aided by numerous corruption scandals. The second wave, which started during Reconstruction and the push West, ended with the great Louisiana lottery scandal of the 1890s.

There wouldn't have to be a scandal at Fort McDowell—which has a pretty clean record, except for allegations of a tip-pool scam. Any evidence of widespread corruption at an Indian casino, combined with moral objections, might be enough to topple the Indians' house of cards.

Gov. Symington's complaints against Indian gambling are both economic and moral. Fort McDowell only pays federal, not state, taxes on its per capita payments and casino payroll. Competition from Indian casinos has hurt the horse and dog tracks, which provide large revenues to the state government. Most gamblers at Fort McDowell are non-Indians who pay state taxes.

"It's a wealth transfer from our economy to theirs," he says. "So on one side of the ledger, we're going to ruin lives. On the other, we're helping Native Americans. Gambling is an unhealthy culture. I consider it to be a very cruel form of taxation.". . .

In Arizona, the individual stories of gambling addiction are harrowing, but Don Hulen of the Arizona Council on Compulsive Gambling admits there are no real statistics for the state. But based on other state studies, he estimates that roughly 5 percent of the state's population has a lifetime predeliction for gambling addiction. He points to an Iowa study where the addiction rate jumped from 1.7 percent to 5.4 percent after riverboat gambling was introduced.

President Pattea's defense is the industry standard. "In this country, we have freedom of choice to do what we want for entertainment. Self-discipline is something maybe a few of them don't have.

"We try to believe it's entertainment," he says.

THE HOPI NATION BALKS AT BLACKJACK

Miriam Davidson

In April 1995, the Hopi Nation voted against establishing gambling operations on tribal-owned lands, Miriam Davidson explains. Those who voted against casinos argue that gaming could have led to compulsive behavior and would have endangered the Hopi tradition of honest work, Davidson writes. On the other hand, she points out, casino supporters contend that an economic boom provided by gaming could have benefited the Hopis. Davidson is a freelance journalist.

The casino gambling business presents an almost irresistible lure for many North American Indian tribes: ready revenues at a time when federal subsidies may be drying up.

It's no secret that Indian-owned gambling enterprises are sprouting on reservations across the nation. Already, about one-third of the 330-plus tribes in the lower 48 states have licenses to operate casino games. And the pace isn't slowing, according to the National Indian Gaming Commission.

But this isn't a lock-step movement.

In April 1995, the Hopi Indians in Arizona joined a handful of American tribes that are choosing not to let their futures ride on the roulette wheel.

But the close Hopi vote—986 were against gambling and 714 for it—underscores the complexity of a decision that often pits a tribe's impoverished living standards and religious and cultural mores against the desire for an immediate source of cash and jobs.

Few Tribes Reject Gambling

Since 1990, when the first agreements between states and tribes were forged allowing casino gambling, only the Hopi and Navajo in Ariz., two other tribes in New York, and one in Texas have explicitly rejected casino gambling, says Linda Hutchinson of the National Indian Gaming Commission.

The Hopis rejected gambling even though the proposed site, on a tribal-owned industrial park near Winslow, Arizona, was more than 60

Reprinted from Miriam Davidson, "Hopis Balk at Blackjack, Dance to Different Drum," *The Christian Science Monitor*, April 19, 1995, by permission of the author.

miles from their reservation. Backers had promised the casino would provide 500 jobs and $15 million in annual revenue for the tribe.

Some Hopi leaders say the vote is proof that their people still value culture and tradition over money. "Our people are taught to work the honest way," says former Hopi Chairman Ivan Sidney. "We believe that we are the last to hold a strong and complete tradition, and that if we fall, it will be the end of Native American traditions in this country."

A former tribal police chief, Mr. Sidney says he has seen how gambling addictions can tear families apart. Rather than ending reliance on government programs, he says, casino gambling replaces one form of dependency with another.

Doubts About Handling Money

Herschel Talashoma, spiritual leader of a windswept village on Third Mesa, says he also urged people to vote against the casino, and not just for cultural reasons. Mr. Talashoma says he doubted the tribal council could be trusted to use the money to benefit all 10,000 Hopis.

Doubts about leadership apparently played a major role in the Navajos' overwhelming rejection of casino gambling in the fall of 1994. Unlike the Hopis, Navajos have no moral or religious qualms about gambling, says Navajo County Supervisor Percy Deal. "I've been at fairs . . . and seen hundreds of Navajo people sitting in circles, playing cards, and betting money."

Mr. Deal wishes the Navajos would reconsider their vote. "There were a lot of scare tactics used—that we would all go crazy, that we wouldn't know how to handle the money," he says. "Well, none of the other tribes that have casinos have gone crazy."

Indeed, many say the jobs and money provided by casinos have reduced, not worsened, social problems on reservations. Rodney Lewis, attorney for the Gila River Indian community south of Phoenix, says the tribes he represents have built fire stations and a nursing home with some of the casino profits and invested the rest. The Gila River Indians plan to open a new casino in May 1995.

"We went into this with our eyes open," Mr. Lewis says, noting that, with pressure building on state governments to compete and on the federal government to regulate, time may be limited for taking advantage of the gaming windfall. "We view it as short-term revenue," he says.

The Need for Economic Development

The Hopi tribe depends on federal payments for about half of its $28 million annual budget, but these funds could soon be cut by Congress. The other main revenue source, a mineral lease to the St. Louis, Mo.–based Peabody Coal Co., is stable but controversial—the company uses groundwater to transport slurry to Nevada. The reservation's remote location, and the culture's emphasis on privacy and self-reliance, have hampered efforts to develop industries like tourism.

Hopi tribal council member Lenora Lewis, a casino supporter, warns that without economic development, young people will be forced to leave the reservation. "I'm glad everyone thought about our culture," she says, "but we need to look to the future too."

ORGANIZATIONS TO CONTACT

The editors have compiled the following list of organizations concerned with the issues presented in this book. The descriptions are derived from materials provided by the organizations. All have publications or information available for interested readers. The list was compiled on the date of publication of the present volume; the information provided here may change. Be aware that many organizations take several weeks or longer to respond to inquiries, so allow as much time as possible.

American Gaming Association (AGA)
555 13th St. NW, Suite 1010 East, Washington, DC 20004-1109
(202) 637-6500 • fax: (202) 637-6507
web address: http://www.americangaming.org
AGA represents the gaming-entertainment industry by addressing regulatory, legislative, and educational issues. The association serves as a clearinghouse for information, develops aggressive educational and advocacy programs, and provides leadership in addressing industry issues that are of public concern, such as problem and underage gambling. AGA publishes the newsletter *Inside the AGA*.

Canadian Foundation on Compulsive Gambling (CFCG)
505 Consumers Rd., Suite 801, Willowdale, Ontario, CANADA M2J 4V8
(416) 499-9800 • fax: (416) 499-8260
e-mail: cfcg@interlog.com • web address: http://www.cfcg.on.ca
An organization of business and health professionals and others, CFCG provides executive summaries of surveys of Ontario residents' attitudes and behavior regarding gambling. It publishes pamphlets on compulsive gambling and teen gambling and has produced a high school curriculum and educational video about problem gambling.

General Board of Church and Society
United Methodist Church
100 Maryland Ave. NE, Washington, DC 20002
(800) 967-0880 • (202) 488-5600 • fax: (202) 488-5619
web address: http://www.umc-gbcs.org
This department of the United Methodist Church believes that "gambling is a menace to society; deadly to the best interests of moral, social, economic, and spiritual life; and destructive of good government." It urges Christians and others to abstain from gambling and opposes state promotion and legalization of gambling. The board provides an antigambling information packet that includes position papers, pamphlets, and article reprints.

Institute for the Study of Gambling and Commercial Gaming
College of Business Administration, University of Nevada
1664 N. Virginia St., Reno, NV 89957
(702) 784-1442 • fax: (702) 784-1057
web address: http://www.unr.edu/colleges/coba/game/
The institute offers courses and degrees in management and other areas of gambling. It holds national and international conferences on gambling and publishes proceedings from them. The institute publishes books and reports

on current issues and trends in legalized gambling and copublishes, with the National Council on Problem Gambling, the quarterly *Journal of Gambling Studies*.

Michigan Interfaith Council on Alcohol Problems (MICAP)
PO Box 10212, Lansing, MI 48901-0212
(517) 484-0016 • (800) 745-3334

MICAP is an organization of religious leaders and others who seek to address the problems of alcoholism. It publishes the biweekly newsletter *MICAP Recap*, which often includes editorials and other information about the negative effects of legalized gambling and opposition to casino gambling in the greater Detroit area.

National Coalition Against Legalized Gambling (NCALG)
110 Maryland Ave. NE, Washington, DC 20002
(800) 664-2680
e-mail: ncalg@ncalg.org • web address: http://www.ncalg.org

NCALG opposes the gambling industry and fights for federal laws curtailing gambling. It also provides research and technical and fund-raising support to grassroots groups battling the expansion of gambling in their states. NCALG publishes a quarterly newsletter.

National Congress of American Indians (NCAI)
2010 Massachusetts Ave. NW, 2nd Fl., Washington, DC 20036
(202) 466-7767 • fax: (202) 466-7797
e-mail: jdossett@erols.com • web address: http://www.ncai.org

NCAI is a tribal organization that represents 600,000 American Indians who seek to protect, conserve, and develop their natural and human resources. NCAI believes that gaming is a right of American Indian tribes and an aspect of tribal sovereignty. It asserts that the 1988 Indian Gaming Regulatory Act was a concession to the federal government and states and believes further concessions are unwarranted. NCAI publishes a quarterly newsletter, the *Sentinel*.

National Council on Problem Gambling
John Jay College of Criminal Justice
445 W. 59th St., New York, NY 10019
(800) 522-4700 • (410) 730-8008 • fax: (410) 730-0669
e-mail: ncpg@erols.com • web address: http://www.ncpgambling.org

The council includes health, education, and law professionals, recovering gamblers, and others concerned with compulsive gambling. It conducts seminars and training programs on the identification and treatment of compulsive gambling behavior. The council publishes books, brochures, videos, the quarterly *National Council on Problem Gambling Newsletter*, and the quarterly *Journal of Gambling Studies*, which explores the psychological behavior of controlled and pathological gamblers.

National Indian Gaming Association (NIGA)
224 Second St. SE, Washington, DC 20003
(202) 546-7711 • fax: (202) 546-1755
e-mail: niga@dgsys.com • web address: http://www2.dgsys.com/~niga

NIGA comprises American Indian tribes that operate bingo games or gambling casinos. It works for the successful operation of Indian casinos as well as effective tribal, state, and federal regulation. NIGA publishes the quarterly newsletter *Moccasin Telegraph*.

North American Association of State and Provincial Lotteries (NASPL)
1700 E. 13th St., Suite 4-PE, Cleveland, OH 44114
(216) 241-2310 • fax: (216) 241-4350
e-mail: nasplhq@aol.com • web address: http://www.naspl.org

The mission of NASPL is to assemble and disseminate information about the benefits of state and provincial lottery organizations. It also works to maintain public confidence and support for state- and provincial-sponsored lottery organizations, believing that these lotteries are important means of generating revenue to meet public needs. NASPL publishes *Lottery Insights* monthly.

BIBLIOGRAPHY

Books

J. Edward Allen   *The Basics of Winning Slots.* Brooklyn, NY: Cardoza, 1997.

Kirk D. Davidson   *Selling Sin: The Marketing of Socially Unacceptable Products.* Westport, CT: Quorum Books, 1996.

Edward F. Dolan   *Teenagers and Compulsive Gambling.* Danbury, CT: Franklin Watts, 1994.

Roger Dunstan   *Gambling in California.* Sacramento: California Research Bureau, 1997.

William R. Eadington and Judy A. Cornelius, eds.   *Gambling Behavior and Problem Gambling.* Reno: University of Nevada Press, 1993.

Rod L. Evans and Mark Hance   *Legalized Gambling: For and Against.* Chicago: Open Court, 1998.

Kathryn Gabriel   *Gambler Way: Indian Gaming in Mythology, History, and Archaeology in North America.* Boulder, CO: Johnson Books, 1996.

Robert J. Hutchinson   *The Absolute Beginner's Guide to Gambling.* New York: Pocket Books, 1996.

International Gaming Institute   *The Gaming Industry: Introduction and Perspectives.* New York: John Wiley and Sons, 1996.

Ambrose I. Lane   *Return of the Buffalo: The Story Behind America's Indian Gaming Explosion.* Westport, CT: Bergin and Garvey, 1995.

Richard McGowan   *State Lotteries and Legalized Gambling.* Westport, CT: Praeger, 1994.

National Indian Gaming Association   *Speaking the Truth About Indian Gaming.* Washington, DC: National Indian Gaming Association, 1993.

David Spanier   *Inside the Gambler's Mind.* Reno: University of Nevada Press, 1994.

William Norman Thompson   *Legalized Gambling: A Reference Handbook.* Santa Barbara, CA: ABC-CLIO, 1994.

Michael B. Walker   *The Psychology of Gambling (International Series in Social Psychology).* Newton, MA: Butterworth Architecture, 1996.

Periodicals

Michael Angeli   "Fleecing Las Vegas," *Esquire,* May 1997.

Sandra Blakeslee   "Suicide Rate Is Higher in Three Gambling Cities," *New York Times,* December 16, 1997.

Marc Cooper   "America's House of Cards: How the Casino Economy Robs the Working Poor," *Nation,* February 19, 1996.

Stephanie Anderson
Forest
"Big Trouble in the Big Easy," *Business Week*, October 16, 1995.

James H. Frey, ed.
"Gambling: Socioeconomic Impacts and Public Policy," *Annals of the American Academy of Political and Social Science*, March 1998.

William A. Galston
and David Wasserman
"Gambling Away Our Moral Capital," *Public Interest*, Spring 1996.

Ted G. Goertzel and
John W. Cosby
"Gambling on Jobs and Welfare in Atlantic City," *Society*, June 1997.

S.C. Gwynne
"How Casinos Hook You," *Time*, November 17, 1997.

Richard G. Hill
"The Future of Indian Gaming," *Cultural Survival Quarterly*, Winter 1994.

Bernard P. Horn
"Is There a Cure for America's Gambling Addiction?" *USA Today*, May 1997.

Margot Hornblower
"No Dice: The Backlash Against Gambling," *Time*, April 1, 1996.

*Issues and
Controversies On File*
"Gambling," January 12, 1996. Available from Facts On File News Services, 11 Penn Plaza, New York, NY 10001-2006.

Timothy M. Ito et al.
"Racing's Rough Ride," *U.S. News & World Report*, June 12, 1995.

Peter T. Kilborn
"For Poorest Indians, Casinos Aren't Enough," *Racefile*, May/June 1997. Available from the Applied Research Center, 1322 Webster St., Suite 402, Oakland, CA 94612.

Martin Koughan
"Easy Money," *Mother Jones*, July 17, 1997.

Michael Krantz and
Dick Thompson
"Cyberspace Crapshoot: The Imminent Boom of Online Gambling Raises a Host of Dicey Moral and Jurisdictional Issues," *Time*, June 2, 1997.

Greg Raver Lampman
"Charlotte's Millions," *Washingtonian*, June 1995.

Anthony Layng
"Indian Casinos: Past Precedents and Future Prospects," *USA Today*, March 1996.

April Lynch
"All Bets Are Off," *Mother Jones*, July 17, 1997.

Joseph Maglitta
"High-Tech Wagering: Jackpot or Jeopardy?" *Computerworld*, February 7, 1994. Available from Computerworld, Inc., 500 Old Connecticut Path, Framingham, MA 01701.

Chip Mitchell
"Casinos for Chiapas," *Progressive*, March 1997.

Timothy C. Morgan
"The Invisible Addiction," *Christianity Today*, April 8, 1996.

Ellen Perlman
"The Game of Mystery Bucks," *Governing*, January 1998.

Brett Pulley
"Casinos Paying Top Dollar to Coddle Elite Gamblers," *New York Times*, January 12, 1998.

Ronald A. Reno	"The Diceman Cometh: Will Gambling Be a Bad Bet for Your Town?" *Policy Review*, March/April 1996.
William Safire	"Losers Weepers," *New York Times*, January 27, 1997.
William Thompson and Diana R. Dever	"A Sovereignty Check on Indian Gaming (Part II): The Downside of the Sovereignty Equation," *Indian Gaming Magazine*, May 1994. Available from 15825 Shady Grove Rd., Suite 130, Rockville, MD 20850.
Richard E. Vatz and Lee S. Weinberg	"Refuting the Myths of Compulsive Gambling," *USA Today*, November 1993.
Michael Ventura	"Site Visit to Las Vegas: The Psychology of Money," *Psychology Today*, March/April 1995.
Wall Street Journal	"Gambling in America," May 10, 1996.
Robert Weissman	"A Bad Bet: Casino Economics and the Politics of Gambling," *Multinational Monitor*, November 1996.
Richard L. Worsnop	"Gambling Boom," *CQ Researcher*, March 18, 1994. Available from 1414 22nd St. NW, Washington, DC 20037.

Index